milton
intellectual property

Canada does not suffer from a shortage of research and Canadians have plenty of innovative ideas. However, Canadians do not have a good track record of successfully commercializing their innovations.

Canadians grew wealthy and happy on natural resource riches, but that era is ending quickly. If we want to avoid becoming bitter and broke, we must rapidly increase commercialization and our production and export of value-added products and services. We are already well behind our economic peers, like Sweden, so we need to move with urgency on this agenda. Swedes file five times as many patents and trademarks per capita than Canadians in the "BRIC" countries (Brazil, Russia, India, and China). Accordingly, the aim of this book is to give you a flavour for the basics of intellectual property law and to help start making your organization "IP Smart."

For information beyond the basics and to find answers to specific questions about patents, trademarks, and copyrights, please consult our IP Wiki: **www.miltonsip.com\wiki**.

I extend my sincere thanks to both the EDC and NRC-IRAP, who have been excellent partners. They had the vision to recognize the importance of increasing awareness of intellectual property and they moved very nimbly to support this book.

Neil Milton

Ottawa, 2010

www.miltonsip.com

Canadian Intellectual Property Law For Dummies,® Special Edition

Published by
John Wiley & Sons Canada, Ltd.
6045 Freemont Boulevard
Mississauga, Ontario, L5R 4J3
www.wiley.com

ISBN: 978-0-470-94159-1

Printed in Canada

1 2 3 4 5 PC 14 13 12 11 10

For details on how to create a custom book for your company or organization, or for more information on John Wiley & Sons Canada custom publishing programs, please call 416-646-7992 or e-mail cupubcan@wiley.com.

For general information on John Wiley & Sons Canada, Ltd., including all books published by Wiley Publishing, Inc., please call our warehouse, Tel 1-800-567-4797. For reseller information, including discounts and premium sales, please call our sales department, Tel 416-646-7992. For press review copies, author interviews, or other publicity information, please contact our marketing department, Tel 416-646-4584, Fax 416-236-4448.

WILEY

Canadian Intellectual Property Law
FOR
DUMMIES®
SPECIAL EDITION

by Henri Charmasson,
John Buchaca,
Diana Byron, and
Neil Milton

WILEY

John Wiley & Sons Canada, Ltd.

Publisher's Acknowledgments

We're proud of this book; please send us your comments at http://dummies.custhelp.com.

Some of the people who helped bring this book to market include the following:

Acquisitions and Editorial

Editor: Robert Hickey

Manager, Custom Publications: Christiane Coté

Project Editor: Lindsay Humphreys

Copy Editor: Kelly Howey

Cartoons: Rich Tennant (www.the5thwave.com)

Composition Services

Vice-President, Publishing Services: Karen Bryan

Project Coordinator: Lynsey Stanford

Layout: Carl Byers, Melissa K. Jester

Proofreader: Caitie Copple

John Wiley & Sons Canada, Ltd.

Bill Zerter, Chief Operating Officer

Jennifer Smith, Publisher, Professional and Trade Division

Publishing and Editorial for Consumer Dummies

Diane Graves Steele, Vice President and Publisher, Consumer Dummies

Kristin Ferguson-Wagstaffe, Product Development Director, Consumer Dummies

Ensley Eikenburg, Associate Publisher, Travel

Kelly Regan, Editorial Director, Travel

Composition Services

Debbie Stailey, Director of Composition Services

Table of Contents

Introduction

●●

*W*elcome to *Canadian Intellectual Property Law For Dummies.* Because intellectual property (IP) law is very complex and constantly evolving, this isn't a how-to manual. Rather, the aim of this book is to introduce you to some of the key features of IP law and to start you on the path of making your business IP-smart.

As we discuss throughout this book, a professional who specializes in IP is an essential member of your team whenever you're dealing with intellectual property matters. Empowered with the knowledge from this book, you'll be better equipped to interact with and instruct your IP professionals — which, happily, will save you both time and money. Additionally, you'll have a clearer idea of how to integrate IP into your business strategy.

About This Book

This book will not make you an IP expert, but we hope it will give you a good understanding of the fundamentals of IP law. We introduce you to the four main types of IP rights: patents, trademarks, copyrights, and industrial designs. We also offer some suggestions that may help you, and your business, profit from these rights.

This book is no substitute for legal advice from a specialized professional. When dealing with IP and IP rights, you may face many thorny legal issues. And, there's only one definitive answer to any legal question: *It depends.* So make sure you obtain competent legal advice.

Foolish Assumptions

Although we've only just met, we've made some assumptions about you. We hope you don't mind. We're supposing that because you've picked up our book, one or more of the following apply:

- You have an entrepreneurial spirit
- You work in a creative field, such as publishing, writing, or computer programming
- You're an inventor, scientist, and/or engineer
- You're a VP or manager of marketing at a mid-sized company
- You're interested in learning more about IP and how your company can benefit from its uses

How This Book Is Organized

Canadian Intellectual Property Law For Dummies is organized so you can easily access the information you need. If you want to curl up and read the entire book, then you're most welcome to. Alternatively, if you have a specific question or area of interest, feel free to jump right to that spot.

Part 1: Understanding Intellectual Property Assets

Part I introduces you to intellectual property and the professionals who can assist you in securing your IP rights. We also show you the basics of the four types of IP and give you advice on how best to protect your rights.

Part II: Profiting from Intellectual Property

Part II talks about enforcing your IP rights to prevent copycats from stealing your profits. We also show you how to monetize your IP rights by licensing them to third parties. Finally, we suggest ways to benefit from other people's IP.

Part III: The Part of Tens

All *For Dummies* books have a Part of Tens, and of course we do, too. In this part, which contains some valuable information in an at-a-glance format, we unravel some misconceptions about IP in general.

Icons Used in This Book

Throughout the book, these little symbols are on the left side of the page. Here's a guide to what they mean:

Draws your attention to some key information worth remembering.

Indicates a piece of useful information designed to make your IP life a little easier.

Alerts you to common mistakes that may trip you up and to other factors that might prove hazardous to your IP health.

Part I
Understanding Intellectual Property Assets

The 5th Wave   By Rich Tennant

In this part . . .

If you're reading this page, you probably have an invention, creative work, trademark, or industrial design that you want to guard against all the copycats out there. Well, you've come to the right place. In this part we give you an overview of intellectual property (IP) and explain why protecting these assets is important.

Chapter 1

Introducing Intellectual Property

*W*elcome to the world of intellectual property, which is abbreviated IP. If you've ever created, invented, or named something that you're selling, then congratulations — you already have intellectual property. And, even better, that IP may be quite valuable. Think about the people who created the Segway scooter or wrote the first *For Dummies* book. Wouldn't it be great if you could cash in on your IP, just like they did? In this chapter we introduce you to the basics of IP so you can begin to get the lay of the land, and discuss how a professional can help you make the most of your IP.

Explaining Intellectual Property

So, what exactly is intellectual property? Through the years, we've encountered many definitions, including "information that has commercial value," "a proprietary product of the mind," and "things protected by patents, copyrights, and trademarks." Although each of these is true, none is quite complete. Here's our favourite:

Intellectual property is an intangible creation of the mind that can be legally protected. Not all intangible creations can be protected; the ones that can are considered IP.

Because it has no physical form, IP can be a confusing concept. We often find it easier to explain by providing some contrasts of what it is and isn't. Intellectual property is *not*

- ✔ The new and wondrous machine you developed in your garage, but the invention embodied in that machine.
- ✔ The marvelously efficient cholesterol-reducing pill you see advertised on TV, but the formula and the process used in manufacturing that pill.
- ✔ The physical portrait that an artist made of you, but the right to reproduce the image in the painting.
- ✔ The riding mower you reluctantly start up every Saturday, but the brand name that embodies the reputation of the product and its manufacturer.

That's what IP isn't. In the rest of this section, we focus on what it is.

Defining IP rights

Intellectual properties are rights, not things. The owner of the rights can enforce them against any third party. The two most fundamental rights belonging to an intellectual property owner are

- ✔ The right to use the property without interference from others, and
- ✔ The right to exclude others from using the property.

Established under a framework created by the state, IP rights vary from time to time, and country to country.

IP rights differ from other property rights, as the following examples illustrate:

- ✔ **IP rights can be used simultaneously by multiple different users.** Many people can use Windows software at once, but only one person can use a chair at one time.

✔ **IP rights don't wear out.** With most IP rights, the more they're used, the greater their value.

✔ **IP rights, as a general rule, aren't enforced by anyone else, such as the police or the government.** You must enforce them yourself, in the country where the infringement takes place.

Think of intellectual property rights as similar to a call option on a stock — you don't *have* to sue someone for infringing on your right, but the option is yours if you want to enforce it (see Chapter 6 for more on enforcing your rights).

Types of IP

Several core categories of IP exist, with each category protecting different rights in different ways. You can use one or more of the following to secure your IP rights:

✔ **Patents:** Obtaining a patent protects your invention from outright thievery. (We discuss patents in Chapter 2.)

✔ **Trademarks:** Adopting a trademark as a brand name keeps it, and its reputation, all yours. (Chapter 3 spills the beans on trademarks.)

✔ **Copyrights:** Holding a copyright shields your artistic expression from copying. (For more about copyrights, check out Chapter 4.)

✔ **Industrial designs:** Registering an industrial design protects the nonfunctional design features of a product. (See Chapter 5 for details on industrial designs.)

Two other categories of rights are relevant to IP: trade secrets and contractual rights. Unlike the rights we describe above, these can be enforced only against people with whom you have a contractual relationship. So, strictly speaking, they're not property rights because they can't be enforced against third parties. But they are important to understanding IP, so we introduce them here:

✔ **Trade secrets:** Keeping a formula or manufacturing process confidential safeguards it against imitators. (Chapter 2 reveals trade secrets.)

✔ **Contractual rights:** Licensing the right to use someone else's invention. (See Chapter 7.)

Consult with a professional to determine the best way to use IP rights to your advantage. If you don't protect your IP assets by securing your rights, you're out of luck. Without protection, anyone can copy, steal, or change your IP asset. The bottom line is that your unprotected IP gives the bad guys a chance to fatten their bottom line.

Considering the Benefits of Protecting Your IP Rights

Developing and protecting your IP rights is important for at least three good reasons:

- ✔ Gaining an edge over your competitors
- ✔ Creating a revenue source
- ✔ Enhancing the value of your business

When properly secured, IP rights offer benefits similar to those of real property: they can be sold, licensed (see Chapter 7), or used by you or your company.

In some businesses, specific rights convey enormous value. For example, having a patent (see Chapter 2) provides pharmaceutical companies a head start of up to 20 years during which competitors can't manufacture or sell the same drug. Aspirin, Tylenol, and Advil all benefitted from this protection. Ultimately, their patents did expire, but the businesses that launched these products endure because of the power of their trademarks (see Chapter 3).

In other businesses, such as those dependent on relationships rather than patentable products, a patent may not be valuable but a client list could be priceless. IP comes into play there, too. You can protect a client list through trade secrets.

An IP professional can help you determine what IP protection your business will benefit from most.

Keeping your competitors at bay

Almost every IP right gives you a way of excluding others from doing something that interferes with or competes against a vital part of your business.

You may think IP protection isn't for you — that you can tolerate competition and still maintain a reasonable income — so instead of paying for IP protection you spend your resources on marketing or some other activity you consider more productive and lucrative. However, we can't conceive of a business that wouldn't benefit from acquiring at least *some* IP rights.

At a minimum, your business can capitalize on the protection afforded by a trade secret program. This can prevent, or at least deter, former associates or employees from using your manufacturing or marketing methods or stealing a customer list. At the other end of the spectrum, acquiring a patent, copyright, and/or trademark can give you a huge competitive advantage in the marketplace, and the legal clout to stifle copycats.

Consider what your competitors can do if you decide *not* to protect some IP rights. Without a barbed-wire fence, your neighbours' cattle would come and drink from your well. After those strays deplete your meagre water resources, your ranch isn't worth its tumbleweeds. Don't let your competitors deplete your IP resources.

Developing a new revenue source

Many businesses think that the only way to monetize their IP is to sell their own product or service directly to customers, from behind a barbed-wire fence of IP protection. However, after you acquire IP rights, you can also generate substantial income by

- ✔ Licensing someone to manufacture your protected product.

- ✔ Leasing your commercial identifier to another organization to market products under your brand name.

- ✔ Franchising other folks to manufacture or sell your goods and services under your guidelines.

All too often these benefits are overlooked, but remember that under these arrangements you earn money any time someone makes, sells, or uses your goods or services. As we discuss in Chapter 7, IP rights can be licensed to many people (including to competitors), in many places, at the same time. In addition, generally the more you license, the more valuable your rights become.

Licensing IP rights is like renting out real estate. You maintain title to the property (the IP assets and rights) while collecting "rent" in the form of *royalties* (see Chapter 7).

Some business ventures limit themselves to securing solid protection for a product or technology and then licensing the IP rights to others. Say a young entrepreneur launches a new line of sporting or casual garments, enhances his product line with an attractive brand name and logo, and then licenses the brand to other manufacturers after it's established. He then gets out of the business — except, of course, for opening envelopes containing quarterly royalty cheques and laughing all the way to the bank.

Alternatively, many businesses choose to maintain focus on their core activities and license out their name for others to use as a way to extend their brand. For example, we recently saw a Revlon hair dryer for sale, but closer inspection revealed that it wasn't manufactured or distributed by Revlon. Revlon was licensing its mark to a third party in the hair dryer business, and collecting royalties on this brand extension. When they're planned and marketed well, IP rights can be an essential part of your product line.

If you want to generate extra income but don't want to give up the business completely, you can maintain the right to continue manufacturing your product by granting *nonexclusive* licences. However, the royalty rate is lower than for an exclusive licence (again, see Chapter 7 for more).

Adding value to your business

When the time comes to sell your business, you can get more for it if your

- ✔ Products are protected by patents
- ✔ Proprietary computer programs are covered by copyrights

    ✔ Brand names are unique, motivating, and not copyable by competitors

    ✔ *Goodwill* — the reputation of the business — is transferable under the business name (that is, it's not your family name)

    ✔ Customer list has remained secret

Generally, you'll realize the most upside from IP when the acquirer can put the IP to bigger or wider use than you can. But you don't have to sell your business to capitalize on its IP-enhanced value. If you need to raise more capital or borrow money, your IP can provide a boost to your net worth, making your stock more attractive to investors and offering additional collateral security for the lender to consider.

Bringing in the Pros

If you're like most people, the idea of hiring a professional, especially one who has "LL.B" tagged after her or his name, sends cold shivers down your spine, puts goosebumps on your arms, and sets your heart palpitating.

Yes, attorneys are expensive, probably even more so than you think, especially if they specialize in intellectual property cases. But hang on, don't panic — we show you ways to mitigate the high cost of professional services.

First, you have to accept that you'll need a professional's services sooner or later. What counts is that you know what kind of help you need and how to get it, and that you know as much as you can about what it is you're getting (and not getting) from the IP process.

Getting the help you need

Let's face it, you need professional help — and no, we're not questioning your mental fitness. You need professional help when diving into IP waters because acquiring and using IP rights to protect and exploit IP assets are essentially legal procedures. And, as you know, laws are inherently characterized by nuances, exceptions, and loopholes. IP laws are no exception. Although you may find it tempting to save money and do it yourself, we equate this approach with do-it-yourself dentistry — possible, but the results are seldom satisfactory.

An IP professional spends years studying this stuff, bringing a level of expertise to the table that others can't easily duplicate. By steering you clear of legal pitfalls, the IP professional saves you the time, grief, aggravation, and expense of having to refile a defective application or other paperwork. More important, a professional makes sure that you don't miss any critical deadlines and lose the opportunity to acquire the IP protection you need.

This book, helpful as it is, is no substitute for engaging the services of a competent IP specialist should the need arise in your situation.

Identifying the right person for the job

Because IP is such a vast and complex field, many professionals limit their practice to narrow specialties, such as patent applications, trademark cases, IP litigation, or entertainment copyright cases. You need to retain the professional most qualified to handle your particular case.

Registered patent and trademark agents

Individuals who specialize in "prosecuting" IP can be accredited by the Canadian Intellectual Property Office (CIPO) as either patent or trademark agents. *Prosecuting* is a fancy word for "going through the application process to get the rights from the government."

Qualifying as a patent agent involves passing a rigorous four-part examination on patent application procedures. Becoming a trademark agent means either passing an exam or, if the individual is a lawyer, swearing an affidavit that the individual has practised under a trademark agent for two years.

Patent and trademark agents can be lawyers, but what matters for prosecution purposes is that they are agents, and many very good agents aren't lawyers. What agents don't do is help with enforcing IP rights (suing people), or licensing or buying and selling IP rights after they have been secured through prosecution. IP lawyers can help you with these things.

For the purposes of this book, we use the phrase *IP profes-sional* to refer to an individual with the appropriate skills and accreditation to assist you with the specific task at hand.

Nonregistered IP attorneys

Certain well-intentioned business and corporate lawyers won't hesitate to tackle IP matters (other than patent applications) — which indeed they are authorized to do but not necessarily competent to handle. Many are very knowledgeable and do their best, but are clearly out of their league when it comes to the latest developments in IP law.

Be especially careful if you approach someone who's not a specialist in the particular area of IP that's relevant to your current needs, whether it's patents, trademarks, or copy-rights; prosecution; enforcement; or licensing. Question the IP professional about her competence and experience dealing with issues like yours — something you should do whenever consulting a lawyer.

Keeping it secret

You may worry that consulting an IP professional jeopardizes the secrecy of your creation, but rest assured that he has a fiduciary duty to retain your confidences, and this duty is of indefinite duration (it never expires). If your IP professional spills the beans, in addition to being in breach of his duty to you he can be in very serious trouble with his licensing body (for instance, the provincial Law Society). For this reason, the fiduciary duty is usually considered "longer and stronger" than any contractual duty of nondisclosure.

In Canada, communications with lawyers are privileged, but communications with patent and trademark agents are not. *Privileged* communications are ones that you can't be com-pelled to reveal to your opponent in litigation.

If you want to discuss something sensitive, such as whether your business infringes on someone else's IP, make sure you do it with an IP professional who is a lawyer and make sure you keep the communication private. If you hold a conversation in a crowded restaurant, or in a room with your accountant, you may be deemed to have waived privilege.

Finding an IP professional

The best and safest way to find a competent IP professional is by referral from someone who has used that professional's services in the past and been satisfied. You do have some other options, though (listed here in order of our preference):

- Ask for a referral from an attorney you know and trust.

- Consult an attorney referral service, such as your local Bar Association.

- Check the Canadian Intellectual Property Office's list of agents in your area, available online at www.cipo. ic.gc.ca.

- Sift through listings of IP professionals in the phone book under *Intellectual Property Law, Patent Attorneys* or *Patent Lawyers, Patents* or *Patent Searches,* and *Trademarks and Copyrights.*

Qualifying an IP professional

To ensure the person you hire is the right one for the job, interview several candidates and ask some hard questions before you make your final decision. Lawyers and agents will gladly supply you with references and samples of their work and answer these questions:

- What is your technical background?

- How long have you been practising in this field?

- Who else, besides you, will be working on my case?

When interviewing patent agents, ask these questions:

- Are you familiar with my area of technology?

- Have you assisted clients in obtaining patents related to my invention?

- How many patent applications have you handled?

- How many patents have you obtained?

Here are some questions to ask trademark agents:

- ✔ How many applications have you handled?
- ✔ Do you have experience dealing with Examiner's Reports?
- ✔ Have you dealt with oppositions?

When interviewing licensing lawyers, be sure to ask the following:

- ✔ Do you draft licences and other IP contracts?
- ✔ Have you dealt with this industry?
- ✔ Do you issue infringement or noninfringement opinions?

Ask a prospective litigation lawyer these questions:

- ✔ Have you conducted cases in similar areas?
- ✔ Have you conducted trials?
- ✔ What is your approach to mediation?
- ✔ How do you resolve cases?

Retaining an IP professional

When you're ready to retain or hire an IP professional, insist on an engagement contract or retainer agreement that clearly spells out all the services, terms, and conditions of your professional relationship.

Here is a partial checklist of the most important things to include:

- ✔ What the IP professional will do for you.
- ✔ Which professional in the firm will handle your case.
- ✔ How much and when you have to pay for the services.
- ✔ What additional costs and fees you may encounter.
- ✔ How you can terminate the agreement and hire another professional.
- ✔ Whom the IP professional will represent: you, your associate or partner, your company, or the man in the moon.

This last point is particularly important. You may ask your IP professional to do something that isn't beneficial to your associate or your company. An eventual conflict of interest that wasn't properly anticipated can lead to, at best, additional time and expense and, at worst, a nasty legal fight.

Working with foreign IP professionals

You must have a representative in every foreign jurisdiction in which you file a patent application, and often for every application to register a mark. Most patent attorneys and agents maintain working relationships with IP professionals in industrialized foreign countries.

In all cases, you need to pay the foreign IP professionals' fees and government charges. Usually, neither you nor your attorney has any control over these costs, but always ask for a rough estimate when you file overseas. Because foreign costs tend to be substantially higher, don't forget to take those expenses into account when preparing your IP budget and laying out your IP protection strategy. (For more about costs, check out the next section.)

Paying the Piper

Legal services are expensive and eat up the lion's share of the money you spend to protect your intellectual property. We give it to you straight here (you may want to be sitting down), but don't panic — we also give you some advice on keeping your IP protection expenses within your budget.

Assessing the costs

Here's the skinny on some hefty prices. Don't be surprised if your IP specialist quotes you hourly rates between $200 and $500. Keep in mind that fees and costs, including government charges, often change and may not be the same in all places.

Despite the temptation to save money, please remember our earlier advice about not flexing your DIY muscles here. Our experience tells us not to rely on what the client has done on his or her own. An IP pro would rather start from scratch than try to unravel the mangled mess of an inadequate patent application.

You can pay for IP professional services in one of three common ways:

✔ An hourly fee

✔ A fixed amount for the whole job

✔ A combination of the two

If you agree to an hourly fee, request a complete estimate of all the costs over the life of the project, such as filing fees, copying and mailing costs, foreign agent charges, and maintenance fees. *Maintenance fees,* also called *annuities,* are paid to patenting authorities during the life of a patent. In some countries, the annuities are due from the date of filing the application. Be prepared for an estimate having a wide range of costs, because it is very difficult at the outset to predict what will happen over the life of the project.

If you're going to pay a fixed fee, ask about other expenses that may not be included, such as government charges, drawing costs, and copying charges. In all cases, clarify how and when you must make the payments.

Managing the expenses

Informing yourself about IP (one of the key goals of this book) and being organized, efficient, and clear about your goals and expectations will dramatically improve the quality of the service you receive from your IP professional, while also keeping costs down.

Your IP professional can help you properly allocate your resources and minimize IP-related expenses. The following is a short list of what she can do for you:

✔ Give you short-term and long-term estimates of all fees and costs.

✔ Show you how to strategically spread the protective measures over a number of years so you don't have to blow the entire budget all at once, and give you time to figure out whether your product really is as good as the famous Tea Kettle whiskey of yesteryear.

✔ Devise the least expensive approach for protecting your intellectual property — such as applying for a copyright, configuration mark, or design patent application instead of a more expensive patent, or by implementing a trade-secret protection program using confidentiality agreements and other procedures.

✔ Tailor your IP protection program to suit your basic needs. (However, if you need to go into the witness protection program, this book won't help.)

✔ Give you some peace of mind and a bill for her services — not necessarily in that order.

Giving up a piece of the action

Fledgling entrepreneurs are often short of cash and eager to offer their IP professional a part of their business, technology, or invention as payment for services. If you're tempted to do so, think about a few things first:

✔ If the IP professional acquires shares, as part owner of your company or its assets he may have some say about how the business is run. Have a clear, written understanding about these matters to prevent a costly dispute.

✔ You don't yet know what your business or IP is worth, so you may be giving up too much for the services you're trying to secure. Later, you may find yourself without enough remaining assets or ownership of the business to obtain the capital and resources you need. Don't sell yourself short; make sure to evaluate the services and IP properly, and make a fair tradeoff.

✔ A part-of-the-action fee arrangement is different from ownership of shares of a company; it may be possible to pay your agent a royalty from revenue. But, as with any commercial arrangement, get the entire financial arrangement in writing and get an opinion from a business lawyer.

✔ Giving a piece of your invention or company to someone must be done in a legal business framework. As with any business relationship, ensure you clearly document the rights and responsibilities of each party. Any payments must comply with applicable laws, including income tax and securities laws. Remember, IP professionals are not business or securities lawyers, and deals of this nature require review by a professional with relevant experience.

Coordinating with Other Professionals

Don't forget to keep your other advisers informed about your IP program.

✔ **Keep your business or corporate attorney aware of all your IP activities.** Give him copies of all your major correspondence with IP professionals. Your patents and marks may be put to good use in some distributorship and representative agency agreements.

✔ **Inform your CA, comptroller, and other bean counters about your IP expenses.** Acquiring a patent or developing a trade secret can have important tax implications, and you don't want to miss lucrative amortization or depreciation deductions. Proceeds from the sale of licensing of an invention may benefit from special taxation rules, and your technological acquisitions and research program may qualify for tax credits.

✔ **Make your PR and advertising agency fully aware of the marks you acquire and register.** Those marks can be effectively put to work in your promotional campaigns. Your advertising and marketing people can play an important role in selecting your commercial identifiers.

Chapter 2

Mastering Patents

. . . .

In This Chapter

▶ Understanding the purpose of patents

▶ Weighing the pros and cons of patents

▶ Passing the three-part patentability test

▶ Determining what rights you have to your invention

▶ Starting the application process

▶ Drafting your application

▶ Prosecuting the application

▶ Going international

▶ Considering what else an IP pro can do for you

▶ Investigating other IP options

. . . .

A patent is perhaps the best known IP right, but it also happens to be the most misunderstood. In this chapter, we untangle for you — one step at a time — the knotty complexity of patents so that you have no doubts about what a patent is and whether you can get one.

Presenting Patents

A *patent* is a temporary, limited legal right granted to an inventor by a government to prevent others from manufacturing, selling, or using his invention. It's a loaded definition. Read it again, focusing on the most important parts:

✔ **Temporary:** Patents last for 20 years, not forever.

✔ **Limited:** The right associated with a patent isn't absolute, but very specifically limited. It's also subject to the right of any other person who happens to own a dominant patent related to the same subject matter.

✓ **Right . . . to prevent:** A patent allows its owner to go to court and ask a judge to stop someone from doing something. But remember, what's good for the goose is good for the gander. An inventor isn't immune from a superior *right to prevent* held by another patent owner, as illustrated in the "Understanding the limits of your rights as a patent owner" section in this chapter.

✓ **By a government:** Patents are granted country by country. If you patent an invention in only one country, then the invention is free for use in most of the world. Canada is a member of two important treaties, the Paris Convention and the Patent Cooperation Treaty, which make filing patents in foreign countries easier.

Patenting your invention doesn't give you the right to *do* anything with the invention. Instead, think of it as veto power over someone else trying to do something with it. A patent allows the owner to stop others from using, manufacturing, selling, licensing, or otherwise exploiting the specifically covered invention. And that may require going to court and paying large legal fees if the infringer isn't deterred by your threat of litigation.

Investigating what your patent can do for your country

The Canadian Intellectual Property Office (CIPO) controls Canada's patent system. Because it gives one person sole control of a possibly important technological application, the patent system is a limited exception to the general free competition and antimonopolistic principles that underline our body of laws. Yet, in a roundabout way, patents still promote competition among all citizens. A patent gives the inventor incentive to disclose his or her invention, thus contributing to general scientific and technological knowledge.

A patent applicant publishes the nuts and bolts of the invention, giving the public knowledge of the invention very early on — as soon as 18 months from the earliest filing date. In return, the owner gets a 20-year head start in exploiting it.

When the patent expires, the owner can no longer prevent anyone from using the invention or manufacturing and selling anything that falls within that previously taboo area of technology — free competition reigns again, and the country is richer for the technology.

Discovering what your patent can do for you

A patent can be a powerful legal tool that affords you, as an inventor, businessperson, or entrepreneur, the sole right to your technology and a competitive edge in the market.

After your patent is granted, you can go into business yourself to practise the invention, free of competition in respect to what you have patented. You can also license your patent rights to someone else. (A *licence* is a lease that allows another party to exploit your invention. In most cases, it's just a promise by the patent owner not to sue the holder of the licence.) If you've invented something really valuable, potential licensees will be lining up for the opportunity to pay you handsome royalties for the right to profit by your invention. Or you can *assign* (sell) the patent outright for a bundle, giving the new owner the patent's exclusive benefits for the remaining term of the patent. (We talk more about licences and assignments in Chapter 7.)

You don't have to register your patent before going into business. If you prefer, you can start a business armed only with your new idea (so long as it doesn't infringe on someone else's IP rights). You'll just be subject to potential competition without the protection of a patent.

Understanding the limits of your rights as a patent owner

Under your patent, you can sue anyone who manufactures, sells, markets, or even uses the invention without your permission. Remember, however, that receiving your patent does *not* give you the right to make or sell your product. Your product may still infringe someone else's patent, and you will have to deal with that problem separately.

Here's an example. Say that Jane has a patent covering a bicycle that happens to have upright handlebars, but Jane's patent is on a bicycle without reference to the type of handlebars. By developing new under-slung handlebars, you've made it more efficient as a racing bike and have been granted a patent covering the improvement. Jane wants to modify her bike according to your invention, but can't do so without your permission. You, on the other hand, can't make or sell the improved bike without her permission (Jane's patent covers all bikes). The solution is to get together and strike a deal. Here are your options:

- ✓ One of you gives the other exclusive permission to use both inventions, paying a fee for such use to the one who withdraws.

- ✓ Each of you agrees not to sue the other and goes into business using the other's invention without exchange of money.

- ✓ Some other combination of terms on which you can both agree.

Considering the Pros and Cons

So you think you have a patentable invention. It bears remembering that applying for a patent is a long, expensive, and uncertain undertaking. We set out some of the advantages and disadvantages of patents, to help you consider whether pursuing a patent is right for you.

Here are the advantages a patent offers:

- ✓ **Broad scope of protection:** Properly drafted by an IP professional, your patent can extend to embodiments and commericalizations beyond your original ideas. Frequently, you'll find that your invention has broader applications than you first realized.

  Consider that lasers were originally invented for scientific research. The original creators never imagined lasers would become so widespread they'd be used to scan a carton of eggs at the grocery store.

- ✓ **Powerful anti-competition tool:** Businesspeople are wary of infringing patents because of high litigation costs and significant damages awards.

✔ **Increase in the value of your business:** A patent portfolio is a must if you want to raise capital.

Not to be ignored, the disadvantages of a patent are the following:

✔ **High costs:** The costs of patenting are high and difficult to predict. Patenting is a continuous process often requiring multiple applications to cover all aspects of the invention and subsequent improvements. And that's without even thinking about enforcing your patent against an infringer.

A very rough guesstimate of costs is $10,000 to $25,000 to draft and prosecute the application in the first country, and $5,000 to $10,000 for each additional country.

✔ **Your secret is out:** You must bare it all in your application, making it easy for others to use your invention as soon as the patent expires or to design around the manner you have claimed in your application.

✔ **Long wait for (relatively) short-lived protection:** The protection lasts, at most, 20 years from your earliest application filing date, but patent offices can take three, four, and even more years to grant a patent.

The first patents for compact fluorescent light bulbs were filed in the early 1970s, but not many were sold until after 2000, when those patents had expired. Of course, later patents on improvements may still be valid or pending.

Testing 1, 2, 3

To qualify as patentable, a patent application not only must be drafted correctly, but the law also requires the invention to pass through a three-pronged *patentability test:*

✔ **Utility:** Practical usefulness — it needs to have a useful function

✔ **Novelty:** Innovativeness — it's gotta be new

✔ **Non-obviousness:** Something that isn't immediately apparent to a knowledgeable but uninventive person

In the following sections, we explore each hurdle the invention must clear and then provide you with a checklist you can use to make sure your invention meets the requirements necessary to receive a patent.

Making yourself useful

The *utility test* determines whether your invention has any use in the real world. This is an easy one. As long as you can dream up some kind of application for your invention, you won't have any problem passing the utility test. Proving before you apply that your invention actually works satisfactorily is a wise move — if it doesn't, your application is invalid. Furthermore, when applying you must include a complete description of how to make your invention work or your patent application will fail.

Developing a novel approach

The *novelty test* confirms that you've developed an original way to solve a problem. Your invention will be compared to everything that has already been created, disclosed, or proposed anywhere in the world, which is called the *prior art.* Each claim that you have made in your patent will be denied if a prior art device, machine, or process includes *all* the basic components of that claim. As a result, claims are often drafted like Russian nesting dolls, starting with a very broad claim and successively narrowing with more specific claims.

The novelty requirements vary from country to country. In Canada, the rule is absolute novelty, with a 12-month grace period to file. This means that no one in the world, with the possible exception of you, can have disclosed the invention before you file your patent application, and that you can file a patent claim up to 12 months after you first publically disclose the invention.

The United States has a *first-to-invent* system, with a 12-month grace period. (In the first-to-invent system, if two inventors file competing patent applications for an invention the patent goes to the first to make the invention, not the first to file the patent.) Many other countries have an absolute novelty requirement, and are first-to-file jurisdictions with no 12-month grace period.

Be careful if you want to apply for international patent rights. In many countries you must file a patent application somewhere in the world *before* you make any public disclosure of your invention (see the "Patenting Internationally" section later in this chapter).

A key component of the novelty test is the disclosure of the invention. The rules for what constitutes disclosure differ from country to country, especially if the invention isn't obvious from just looking at your product. In Canada, you aren't considered to have disclosed your invention unless the observer can understand it, but this isn't the case in the U.S., where even casually showing your prototype to your neighbour may constitute disclosure.

Generally, you don't lose the patent rights to your invention when you disclose it to someone who owes you a duty to retain the invention in confidence. This includes your lawyer and patent agent (who both owe a fiduciary obligation of confidentiality, which is stronger and longer than any contract) and others who have signed nondisclosure agreements with you. However, note that if someone breaches an obligation of confidence and discloses your invention, your patent rights against the world may be lost, and all you'll be left with is a claim for damages against the discloser.

Avoiding the obvious

To pass the non-obviousness test, the difference between your invention and the prior art must not be obvious to a person with ordinary skill in the relevant field. The problem with this test is defining this mythical person with ordinary skill in your field, who knows everything but isn't inventive. For example, he isn't a typical weekend do-it-yourselfer or a Nobel Prize winner, but an uninventive technician who magically knows, or has access to, all prior art information in the field of the invention.

Your invention probably isn't obvious if it provides a solution to a long-standing problem in an offbeat way or, as the courts like to put it, by *teaching away* from the prior art.

Assessing What You Have

The first step in attempting to protect an invention or other technological breakthrough is determining what rights you have to it. Be prepared for some surprises.

Defining the invention in writing

At first glance, preparing a written description of your invention may seem like a childish exercise — but it's what the pros do to sharpen their understanding of the invention, so follow their lead. Go over your notes, drawings, and models and write down an accurate description of what's new about your invention. Be as concise as possible — 15 lines at the most. Keep your focus on what makes the invention new and unique. Help yourself by sketching the essential aspects of your invention with cross-reference numbers that refer back to the written description.

Focus on describing the nuts and bolts of the invention — how it's made and how it operates, rather than its advantages and commercial applications. Keep in mind that you're not drafting a brochure or technical paper, you're drafting a definition that will become the cornerstone of your patent application. So make sure it's technically accurate and complete. This description is also exactly what a professional needs to conduct your novelty search (see "Searching and surfing" in this chapter).

Qualifying the invention

Determining whether your invention qualifies for a patent is as easy as applying the three-part patentability test and reviewing the checklist of patentability criteria. Check out "Testing 1, 2, 3" for details.

If your innovation ticks all the boxes favourably, then you're in good shape; otherwise, it's back to the drawing board.

Coming up with an inventor

Be brutally honest in assessing whether you alone conceived the invention, or whether someone else made suggestions or contributions to the concept. Did anyone else refine or improve the device when you built the prototype or model? Maybe a co-worker or your 10-year-old whiz kid helped out.

Regardless of the circumstance, make sure you acknowledge any helpful outside contribution now. Any contributor may have rights equal to yours, and therefore must (by law) be listed as a co-inventor on your application.

If you fail to name co-inventors on your patent application you run the risk, especially in the U.S., of having your patent invalidated.

Figuring out ownership

Determining ownership of a patent is related to, but still separate from, inventorship. Patent rights can be bought and sold, both before and after a patent is granted, so often the owner is different from the inventor. The first owner of the patent is named as the applicant on the patent application, and the inventors are named separately. Basically, the inventor owns the rights in an invention if no other circumstances exist. If you have co-inventors, then you have co-owners. If you were employed to create the invention with the understanding that the rights would belong to your employer or customer, then the employer or customer is entitled to own the rights.

Having clear paperwork that establishes ownership and any other rights and obligations in relation to a patent is crucial. Your IP professional can draft an invention and patent transfer agreement for your particular circumstances. The document will be valid regardless of whether it's registered with the Patent Office. However, registering it while your application is pending is wise, because then the patent will issue in your name only.

If you're an employer, take care that your employees don't end up patenting concepts you'd like to use yourself. See an

IP professional, generally a lawyer, for guidance, and make sure to consider the following:

- ✔ **You can tailor your employment intake forms to include invention-assignment clauses.** With these agreements, even an invention outside of your technological field that's made entirely at home with the employee's own resources can be captured by the boss.

- ✔ **All contracts signed with independent entities that are going to develop products for your company should address the issue of ownership of any resulting inventions.** If you don't do this, the contractor will own the patent rights. The terms of any contract should address ownership expressly, as well as the terms of any cross-licences, if one of the parties insists.

- ✔ **If the invention was developed as part of a university project or under a government grant, the government may be due a piece of the action.** Accordingly, you should carefully explore the role of government at the outset.

Addressing ownership issues early in the game lessens the likelihood that you'll run into problems later. When your patent is a success, you may find your consultant or former employee will claim a piece of the action.

Applying for Patent Rights

Absolute novelty is a big deal around the world, and the sooner you file a patent application the better, because this establishes your priority date. The *priority date* is the earlier of either the date that you first file a patent application, or the date when you disclose your invention. Your priority date is important for

- ✔ Proving you've filed a patent application in time,

- ✔ Establishing the relative priorities between competing applications that disclose the same invention, and

- ✔ Determining numerous different international deadlines for filing and paying fees that you must meet in the patent application process.

Two schools of thought exist on the proper approach to applying for patent registration: The first advocates filing as quickly as possible and then conducting a search for prior art; the second prefers conducting a thorough search and then filing.

Although both approaches have pros and cons, we believe that the best approach is a hybrid, which we outline here:

1. File a provisional patent application as quickly as possible, with or without a prior search.

2. Conduct a search if you haven't done so already. (The "Searching and surfing" section in this chapter provides more details on the prior art search.)

3. File a complete patent application before the first anniversary of your priority date.

Provisional applications

Canadian patents are awarded on a *first-to-file* basis, which means that submitting your application as early as possible is essential. CIPO allows you 12 months from your initial application date to revise your application. We encourage you to file a *provisional patent application* as soon as you can. This quick and dirty application essentially marks your spot in line and allows you to preserve your patent rights from the earliest possible filing date. You can use the 12-month window to polish your final specification.

Be aware, however, that real limits to the quality of your rights exist under a provisional patent application. For example, in Canada, failing to amend the application within the first 12 months means that your provisional application will proceed to examination as filed, and will likely lead to weak or narrow rights; in the United States, it leads to your application expiring.

Provisional patent applications are gaining popularity. You can expect to pay approximately $2,500 to $5,000 for yours. Having your IP professional conduct a search before you file your patent application will help to improve the quality of the application and focus the claims, but it's not necessary to conduct one before filing a provisional application.

Searching and surfing

Because novelty is hugely important, searches of prior art are a key component of the patent system. Performing a prefiling search before you apply for registration isn't mandatory, but it's certainly prudent. By reviewing existing patents, technical books, and other relevant publications, you can save yourself a lot of money and potential embarrassment. And your search results will help you and your IP professional submit a better (and cheaper) application.

We strongly recommend that you put some time and energy into conducting searches by yourself. This will help you gain an understanding of the relevant prior art, patenting and the patent system generally, and how you can use other people's IP to your advantage (see Chapter 8). The best place to begin your search is at the U.S. Patent Office Web site (www.uspto.gov). Both the tools and records found at the USPTO site are more extensive than those accessible at the CIPO Web site (www.cipo.ic.gc.ca). Don't worry, though: both sites are structured to be user friendly.

Searching on both sites is keyword based, which sounds good at first but all too often yields spotty results. You see, unfortunately most patents aren't written by normal people. Eccentric IP professionals write them, so instead of describing a spring as . . . well . . . a *spring,* these wacky characters are more likely to call it a *resilient biasing member.* Make sure to include a lot of synonyms in your keyword search (keep a the-saurus handy). And remember, you're not looking for a prior patent showing every detail of your invention, but something that is similar or that suggests one of its main features.

Although you should conduct a preliminary search, relying solely on the results of your DIY searching is a bad idea. We strongly recommend using qualified IP professionals to

> ✔ Conduct fulsome searches before you file a full patent specification,
>
> ✔ Interpret the results of the search, and
>
> ✔ Correlate the results with your invention.

A reasonable estimate of the cost of a properly conducted prior art search is $1,500 to $3,000, which includes a modest amount of interpretation and analysis.

Our preferred approach is to conduct a search either immediately prior to, or — when time is tight — immediately after, filing a provisional patent application. The search may confirm that your invention isn't patentable, and save you a lot of grief. Often, the information you gain from the search will substantially improve the quality and focus of the application that you file. In fact, sometimes a search conducted immediately after a provisional application discloses enough information that it's worthwhile filing another provisional application.

Your prefiling search must look at everything you disclose, teach, or suggest in your claim. And anything that even partially anticipates your invention is a problem.

Proceeding with the Application

Applying for a patent is a complex process, and if you take our advice you'll let your IP professional guide you through most of it. You're not off the hook, though; after all, no one knows your invention better than you, so you should be an active co-participant in preparing the application.

Being at the front of the line

The CIPO employs a first-to-file priority system to deal with competing applications. If someone else files for the same invention before you do, you're out of the game. Applying for a patent as soon as possible is advisable. Indeed, avoid waiting until you work out all the minute details; the CIPO allows you an entire year after your initial filing date to upgrade and consolidate all your ideas into a single, final application, so long as you didn't publish your idea before the initial filing date. Starting with a provisional patent application in the United States gives you the same benefit there.

Filing early is particularly important if you believe that others are working on the same area of technology. Your application filing can serve as a spoiler that prevents theirs from advancing.

Drafting the document

Completing a patent specification (application) involves providing a great deal of detailed information about your invention. Your IP professional can guide you in respect to most of the details, including:

- ✓ **Title:** This'll be short and to the point, and should relate to the article that incorporates the invention.

- ✓ **Field of invention:** Lists the area of technology that applies to your invention (used for indexing purposes).

- ✓ **Background of invention:** Sets the stage for your genius by describing the problem your invention overcomes.

- ✓ **Summary of invention:** Here's where you get to brag about your achievement, and explain your advance over what others have done.

- ✓ **Summary of drawings/figures:** Briefly outlines any attachments that facilitate the understanding of your invention.

- ✓ **Description of preferred embodiments:** Provides one or more examples of the best ways to practise your invention.

- ✓ **Abstract:** Summarizes what your invention is all about.

- ✓ **Drawings or figures:** These complement and support your description of the preferred embodiments.

- ✓ **Claims:** This section defines your rights under the patent. (See more in "Defining your claim" next.)

Focus on assisting your patent professional with the three most important areas of the application — creating your claim, explaining your invention, and providing a detailed description.

Defining your claim

As the inventor, you (with the guidance of your IP professional) are responsible for defining your exclusive rights. A *claim* defines the exclusive rights granted to a patent owner. Completing your claim involves creating a numbered list of features that collectively specify your contribution to humanity.

Functioning as a sort of checklist for infringement, the claim identifies the presence of your invention and specifies what you want to claim as your exclusive rights.

Keep it short and sweet. When drafting your application, you're allowed to make as many claims as you like; however, we recommend you make some of these claims as concise as possible. A claim defines what others can't do, and you can pursue only those infringers who violate every feature listed in a claim. The shorter the claim, the broader the coverage. Don't go any further until you have fully grasped this concept. Please, repeat after us:

> Short claim = more coverage = broad patent
>
> Long claim = less coverage = narrow patent

Keep in mind that your patent coverage may be broader or narrower than you anticipate. Determining what a patent actually covers requires a complex, expert analysis by your IP professional.

Summarizing your invention

Explain what's new and special about your invention. Maintain focus on your specific innovation; don't describe the entire object if you adapted only a portion of it.

Describing your invention

Provide a detailed description of your invention, including figures or drawings whenever they'll be helpful.

Prosecuting the Application

After you've applied for a patent, you begin the process of prosecuting the patent application. *Prosecution* may sound scary, but it simply means following through on your application.

In Canada, filing a Declaration of Entitlement within three months of submitting your application is one of the first steps in prosecuting the application. This process establishes the claim of the applicant, as owner, to the patent application. Then, assuming you've completed your application correctly, little will happen for a number of years unless you press the action (you know — push the examiner forward rather than waiting patiently for your turn).

If you've filed in Canada, then on the second anniversary of your filing date you must begin to pay annual maintenance fees. These will be required yearly during the remaining 20 years that your patent is active. Other countries also require the payment of maintenance fees. In the United States, the fees are due less frequently but are in larger amounts.

You must request an examination within five years of filing your application in Canada. Given the current number of pending applications, you'll wait about two years for the results of your examination. It's often a good idea to take advantage of the five-year window. You likely have applications pending in other jurisdictions, particularly the U.S. You and your patent agent will learn a great deal from your experiences with these other patent offices. You can use this knowledge to amend your Canadian claims to conform with ones that have been approved by foreign offices. Generally, if you inform the examiner of foreign approvals, you'll have an easier time obtaining Canadian approval.

During the examination process, the examiner issues a Patent Office Search Report and an Examiner's Report (commonly known as the office action) containing objections and commentaries from the patent examiner. The office action advises you what's required in order for your patent to be granted. Often, some objections from the examiner will be simple technical concerns as to general wording in the patent specification. Other objections will be directed to the claims with reference to the prior art, accompanied by a requirement that the claims be made more specific. Every applicant also has an opportunity to amend his application to make grammatical corrections to the story and to refine the scope of the claims.

In Canada, this procedure of responding to the examiner's objections frequently goes through two or three cycles, so be patient. Remember, in principle you have to go through the same examination process in each country where you have filed a patent application, so it makes sense to develop a streamlined and efficient response process.

If you overcome all of the examiner's objections, your application will be allowed; if you can't overcome them all, your application will be rejected. In Canada, for a successful application you'll have six months to pay the final government fee and to record any assignments that you want in place at the time the Canadian patent is issued. The patent will be issued in the name of the assignee on record at the time of issue.

Patenting Internationally

Filing international patent applications is important for Canadians. It's a big world, and for many products Canada and the United States represent only a small portion of the potential market. Protecting your rights internationally is vital. You may choose to patent in countries where you expect to sell your product, in countries where you think you have a prospect of licensing your patent rights, or in countries where infringement is common.

Pursuing patents in the United States

Consider applying for protection in the U.S., because it's a major market for many Canadian businesses. The U.S. economy is more than 10 times larger than ours, and if you do business there your U.S. patent could be correspondingly more valuable than your Canadian one.

Canadians often choose to file their U.S. patent application prior to filing in Canada, and as a result many Canadian patent agents are also licensed to practise before the USPTO and can assist Canadians by filing and prosecuting applications there. Your IP professional will guide you through the U.S. patent process, but we'd like to point out one of the key differences between Canadian and U.S. patent law so you can prepare accordingly:

United States patent law reserves patents for the first inventor. To preserve U.S. rights in the event of a conflict with another applicant, it's essential that you make records of your invention(s) as you proceed. (We use the expression *invention(s)* because you'll be surprised at how the nature of the invention grows over time.)

As you develop your product or process, take copious notes that include plenty of illustrative sketches, preferably in a bound notebook with numbered pages — after all, that's what Edison did. Use a pen, not a pencil, and don't erase your mistakes, cross them out. Once in a while, ask a trusted relative or friend to review your notes and date and sign the last written page, stating that on the specified date she or he read the notes and understood the invention. This will serve you well if you have to defend against potential interference in respect to your U.S. application.

Because Canada is a first-to-file country, keeping these kinds of records isn't necessary to obtain a Canadian patent. Effectively, the law here treats an invention as not yet invented until an application has been filed at the Canadian Patent Office, or at some other Patent Office in the world from which priority is claimed. However, be aware that if your Canadian patent ever goes into litigation, your opponent will want to know the history of the idea's development. They'll investigate every nook and cranny in the hope that they might discover you're not the true inventor of the idea — because that would invalidate your Canadian patent. Therefore, keeping good records that are up to the U.S. standard is in your best interest, whether or not you file there.

Going global

Patenting is expensive, but protecting your rights is essential if you do business globally. Patent applications must be filed in each country where you want protection, and your costs increase with each application filed. So, determining where to file is one of the most vexing capital allocation decisions the management of an innovative company can face.

As you try to decide whether or not to apply for a patent in Lower Slobovia, ask yourself two key questions:

- ✔ Will the patent make a difference to how much revenue we can generate in Lower Slobovia?

- ✔ Will we (or a licensee) have the money and desire to enforce the patent in Lower Slobovia?

If Lower Slobovia is a small market, or has a weak judicial system, you might decide to spend your IP resources elsewhere. Also, don't feel that you have to file a patent in a country where you fear infringers may create knock-offs of your products. If the real market for those products is elsewhere, then you should pursue patent protection where the products will be sold, not where they're created.

Benefitting from treaties

Canada is a member of two treaties that make it easier for you to apply for international patents: the Paris Convention of 1883 and the Patent Cooperation Treaty. The Paris Convention allows member countries from around the world to accept patent applications from citizens of other member countries. With close to 200 members, this opens up a world of possibilities. The Patent Cooperation Treaty (PCT) doesn't produce patents, but rather is a central processing system you can use during an interim stage of the patent application process. Rather than applying to many different countries, you can initially make a single filing in the PCT system, which reserves your right to file that application in any member nation.

As a Canadian, you can enter the PCT when you submit your original patent application, or just before the end of the priority year, claiming the benefit of your first priority filing date. Either way, you must exit from the PCT system by filing your patent applications in the desired foreign countries within 30 (or 31) months of the earliest priority date associated with your filing (meaning you can't use the PCT as an indefinite placeholder).

Filing a single PCT application allows you to postpone filing overseas while still retaining a priority date from your initial PCT application — key in any first-to-file jurisdictions. PCT applications provide a number of other benefits, including:

- ✔ **Receiving a well-done international search report as of 16 months from your earliest priority date.** (Actually, this can take a little longer in countries with large backlogs, such as the United States.)

- ✔ **Having an opportunity to amend your claims within two months of receiving the international search report.** This means you can make one amendment that will count for all destination countries. Imagine the time and financial costs you'll incur if you file separately and have to amend multiple applications.

✔ **Obtaining a preliminary examination.** For an extra fee, a PCT examiner will produce a Preliminary Examination Report. The report is nonbinding in any of the destination countries, but it provides you, and your investors, with feedback about your prospects for obtaining patent protection. The deadline for filing for Preliminary Examination is month 22 from your priority date. You are allowed to amend both the claims and the disclosure (to correct grammatical errors) during Preliminary Examination.

✔ **Retaining the right to operate in English or French while you're within the PCT system.** This means that if your Preliminary Examination reveals your chances of obtaining a patent are slim and you decide not to go ahead, you've saved yourself the cost of translating your patent application (which can be very expensive). If you do decide to file in a particular country, you must file in its native language.

Your application will be published in printed form and then distributed around the world as of 18 months from your earliest priority date. It will also be available over the Internet at the PCT Web site, www.wipo.int/pctdb/en. You may argue that this isn't such a good thing, because publication of your application will end its secrecy. However, applications filed in most countries around the world are now published as of 18 months from the earliest priority date, so the PCT system is no different. If you wish to preserve your first priority date, you'll have to accept that your PCT application is going to be published.

Using the PCT to defer your patent application while maintaining your priority date allows you to keep your rights alive and your options open, while delaying expenditures as much as possible. Additionally, your knowledge of both your invention and the potential market for your product will improve over time, so deferral allows you to submit a better application.

Taking advantage of the PCT process is a complex but worthwhile endeavour that's best left to the pros. Consult an IP professional about your situation.

Beyond Applications

Patent professionals don't simply file patents for new inventions — they also use their relevant expertise to provide different IP opinions, including the following:

✔ **Infringement opinion:** If you're concerned about infringing on someone else's turf by selling your own thingamajigs, or if you're concerned that someone else is infringing your patent, ask an IP professional to provide an infringement opinion.

Determining whether you're infringing someone else's patent involves predicting what invention you might be infringing upon — which is no easy task. Your IP professional will search all unexpired patents and pending applications for any claims that potentially overlap with your product or process. If this infringement search locates a patent with an independent claim that you appear to be infringing upon, you must either change your product or challenge the validity of the patent. Similarly, you require an infringement opinion before suing anyone for infringement of your own patent.

✔ **Validity analysis:** If you're accused of violating a patent, you may be able to defend yourself by disputing the *validity* — the legal soundness — of the patent. Your IP professional scrutinizes the patent that you're violating, and its application, for errors, but validity searches mainly focus on the role of the examiner — did he do a good job? If your IP professional can challenge the validity of the patent, then you may be in luck. For instance, perhaps there was prior art that predates the patent in question, which invalidates the patent.

If you can't invalidate the patent, you may need to change the configuration of your product or approach the patent owner for a licence (see Chapter 7).

✔ **Freedom-to-operate analysis:** Your IP professional attempts to establish that you can conduct your business as you intend to, without infringing anyone else's patent rights. This is an expensive and time-consuming analysis and, unfortunately, it's impossible to conclusively prove that you're free to operate, so this analysis can only reduce your risk, not eliminate it.

But remember, just because something's difficult or expensive doesn't mean it's not worth doing. Research In Motion encountered difficulty with NTP when the BlackBerry email software inadvertently infringed on a pre-existing patent belonging to NTP. A freedom-to-operate analysis might have disclosed the existing NTP patent and helped prevent very costly litigation.

✔ **State-of-the-art search:** Inventor-initiated research and development programs often use these searches to gain expertise in a technical field. Your IP professional conducts very detailed and technical searches of electronic databases, Web sites, and literature from technical libraries. A state-of-the-art search nearly always produces interesting information to help you improve your understanding of your own invention.

✔ **Patent title search:** If you need to find the name of a patent owner, a patent title search is helpful. Although it's not a legal requirement to record an ownership interest in a patent, many people do. The CIPO keeps track of all recorded assignments and other recorded transactions relating to patents or pending applications.

Exploring Alternatives

Given the length and expense of the patent application process, you should understand some alternative, less-taxing approaches for protecting your invention. You may want to use one or more of those approaches rather than, or in addition to, the patent application.

Keeping secrets

If you're dealing with a chemical or process invention, or other invention that you don't have to expose to your customers or the general public, and can keep it under your hat, then a patent application may not be the best approach for you.

Instead, consider the option of a trade secret strategy. If your invention is to be protected as a trade secret, then it must genuinely be a secret, even within your own organization. Employees must sign secrecy or confidentiality agreements, and the techniques or technologies involved with your invention must not be apparent to visitors at your facilities.

If someone takes advantage of you and improperly acquires knowledge of your concept, you must satisfy a court that you were trying to maintain a trade secret. If you do, the court issues a restraining order, preventing the bad guys from exploiting your idea. However, if the secrecy is spoiled and anyone can understand your technology, then you lose control over the secret. Your only recourse is to seek compensation in the form of damages from whoever broke their duty of secrecy.

Another risk associated with trade secrets is that someone else may independently discover the same invention that you've been keeping secret. They're free to compete with you. In fact, they might even file a patent application and cause you considerable grief by shutting you down.

Generally, pursuing the trade secret route is a good idea if the useful life of your invention is relatively short: less than seven years. The odds of anyone discovering and patenting the same invention during that timeframe are small, and you'll have achieved a head start on the competition.

Backing up your trade secret with a covert patent application isn't common, but it can be an effective strategy if you think your invention will give you a competitive advantage for more than seven years. Patent applications are initially held in secrecy for up to 18 months from the date of your initial filing. If you've managed to keep your invention a secret for those 18 months, you can withdraw the patent application so that it's not published. You can then begin the process again.

Publishing to poison the well

Publishing your invention without filing a patent application means you'll likely lose your right to patent, but because prior art now exists you also can bar anyone else from ever filing a patent on the same invention. This technique relieves you of the cost of patenting, and puts everyone on a level playing field.

Publishing the invention can be as simple as putting it on your Web site. Another very effective method is filing a provisional Canadian patent application, which allows CIPO to publish the invention. After it's been published, you can abandon the application. This tactic allows you to produce a publication that every competent patent searcher in the world will find in her search of the prior art.

In certain circumstances, other alternatives to patenting exist, including industrial design protection (see Chapter 5) and copyright protection (refer to Chapter 4). Whether or not they're a viable option for you depends greatly on your specific circumstances — consult an IP professional.

Chapter 3

Tackling Trademarks

*W*hen you start a business or introduce a new product or service, you have an opportunity to create value out of nothing. By selecting a strong and effective identifier, you gain protection for your enterprise and the chance to catapult your products or services into a dominant market position.

In this chapter we bring you the basics of trademarks, including valuable advice on choosing a distinctive, legally protectable name.

Making Your Mark

Everyone's familiar with brands. You probably even have your own favourites: names that make you reach out for a particular product instead of the others on the shelf. That's the power of a brand — it lends personality to products and services, and creates an association in the mind of the consumer. Trademarks allow you to harness the power of that association so that only you can benefit from it.

Trademarks are symbols, words, logos, or shapes that differentiate your ware (in the trademark business, products are referred to as *wares*) or service from its competitors. When you've established your trademark, you're entitled to defend it from imitators (see the "Enforcing Your Mark" section in this chapter).

Trademarks can be broken down into the following categories:

- ✔ **Ordinary marks** are the words, logos, or symbols that make your product or service stand out from the competition. For example, the word Nike and the swoosh logo make Nike shoes noticeable on the shelf.

- ✔ **Distinguishing guise** is the packaging or design of a product that helps to distinguish it from others — such as the unique shape of a Coca-Cola bottle.

- ✔ **Certification marks** single out products or services meeting a particular standard (for example, CSA stickers on a bike helmet or a professional designation such as CMA or CFP). The owner of a certification mark doesn't make wares or services available directly to the public; instead it certifies the quality of a ware or service provided by a third party. The owner of the mark (the licensing body) controls the use of the mark by its licensees.

- ✔ **Official marks** are owned by entities under government control. (See the sidebar "Being official" for more information.)

- ✔ **Geographic indications** control the use of specific geographic locations as trademarks. Only products originating from a certain region can bear a trademark of that region. For example, sparkling wine can be called *Champagne* only if it originates in the Champagne region of France. As globalization continues to expand and cheap imitations arise, this area of trademark protection will grow in importance.

Although they sound similar, a trademark is not the same thing as a trade name. Your *trade name* is the name under which you carry out your business. Contrary to popular belief, registering your trade name doesn't protect it from use by others. The good news is that you can also register it as a trademark, but only if you're using it as one. (For more about registering trademarks, see the section "Taking the Next Steps.")

Being official

In Canada, entities that are under the direction of the government can apply for "official marks." Official marks are enormously powerful because they don't undergo any examination, no opposition by third parties is possible, and they effectively trump prior registrations by private-sector parties.

The range of organizations that can apply for official marks might surprise you. "Controlled by government" has been interpreted quite broadly by the courts. For example, the courts determined the Canadian Olympic Association was entitled to file official marks.

Organizations that can file official marks include hospitals, universities, community colleges, municipalities, and their spin-off entities, and these entities should all be taking active steps to protect their marks from unauthorized use by third parties. For example, if you're starting a charitable foundation to support your local hospital, both you and the hospital should get advice from an IP professional about your respective trademark rights. However, if you operate a for-profit business and run up against an official mark, you should consult your IP professional and seriously consider changing your mark.

Distinguishing Yourself from the Competition

Creating a distinctive brand makes your business more valuable and your trademark rights easier to enforce. The name you create will fall into one of five main categories; we list them below, in order from best to worst.

- ✔ **Invented marks** are the best kind to have for your business. They didn't exist before you made them up, so they are inherently distinctive. (Existing examples include Kodak, Exxon, Cisco.)

- ✔ **Arbitrary marks** exist in the dictionary because they're genuine words. They're considered arbitrary in this case because they don't refer specifically to the character or quality of your product. (Existing examples include Indigo, Apple, Roots.)

✔ **Suggestive marks** allude to the nature of the product or service, without fully describing it. (Existing examples include Whirlpool for washing machines, Chapters for book stores.)

✔ **Personal names** are very common, and yet they aren't a good choice for a trademark. Remember, the key to a good mark is distinctiveness — likely nothing is unique about your name, so it's very hard to register.

✔ **Descriptive marks** are the weakest kind you can adopt. Terms such as "click" for a camera or "clean and fast" for a dry cleaner are difficult if not impossible to register, and may not be enforceable; after all, almost everyone in your industry could lay claim to the same terms.

When choosing your trademark, don't pick something that someone else will object to. Don't select "Orange Crash" for your new soft drink — you're only asking for trouble from the good people at Orange Crush. Even if you're able to defend your choice of mark, who needs the distraction and expense of litigation? You've got a business to run and products to launch.

The key feature of a trademark is that it makes your product or service stand out from others available on the market. Your reputation develops over time, as the combination of a good product and a memorable trademark generate good-will with your customers. Customers continue to buy your products and spread the word about your services, and this goodwill brings in additional customers. The first step in developing this reputation is creating a quality product or service. A close second is choosing your mark carefully. Make sure to select something that reflects your identity and highlights your uniqueness.

Selecting your mark is a little like flirting — you want to be suggestive, not obvious. Anything too descriptive is a no-no. You can't call your ice cream "Cold & Tasty" because the courts won't take away the freedom of others to use these basic descriptors. And if you're hoping to stand out from the crowd, calling your new hotel "Sandy Beach Resort" won't do. It's immediately obvious to potential customers what and where you are, but what's the difference between your hotel and all the others that are located on sandy beaches? You'd never be able to claim trademark rights because the name is so broad and descriptive that it lacks distinctness.

Avoiding travel sickness

If you plan to market your wares in foreign markets, you must choose your mark even more carefully. Ensure your identifier travels well and doesn't evoke something morbid, ridiculous, or obscene in the foreign idiom:

✔ In Japanese, the word *shi*, which means four, has the same sound as the word for death. The Korean word *sa* has a similar problem. Avoid them both when branding a product to be exported to Asia.

✔ The mark for Nova on a car, with a simple switch of emphasis to the last syllable, means "it won't go" in Spanish.

✔ In Germany, the term *mist*, as in the curling iron mark Mist Stick, stands for *manure*.

✔ The French word *camelote* means shoddy merchandise.

✔ When the slogan used to promote Parker pens — "It won't leak in your pocket and embarrass you" — was translated into Spanish, it read, "It won't leak into your pocket and make you pregnant."

Globalization requires that commercial identifiers be acceptable in any market where they might be introduced. We recommend you consult an international dictionary of obscenities to prevent any embarrassment overseas.

 Writing some sample advertisements is a good exercise that can help you avoid this pitfall. Remember, your mark should identify your product and make it stand out from the competition; it shouldn't describe it. Consider the difference between "use Turtle wax next time you shine your car" and "use Glossy wax next time you shine your car." See how easily you can spot potential trouble this way?

Taking the Next Steps

As with all IP rights, establishing ownership is crucial. Business owners commonly make the mistake of hiring a contractor to assist with developing a trademark, especially logos and designs, and then failing to get an assignment of the copyright from the contractor. The technical term for this situation is *a mess,* and it can be easily avoided by obtaining clear paperwork upfront.

After you carefully craft your trademark and ensure you have ownership of it, you need to get moving. Canadian law operates on a first-come, first-served basis with respect to trademarks. In other words, priority goes to the first person to adopt the trademark.

As we're sure you know, laws are often complicated and confusing — why should trademark laws be any different? Below we explain the basic steps involved, but we can't possibly cover all the complex aspects of registering and protecting a mark. We encourage you to spend some of your branding budget on consulting with an IP professional who specializes in trademark law. He or she will be able to guide you through the intricate legal issues that lie ahead.

Deciding whether to register

In Canada it's not necessary to register your trademark in order to lay claim to it; you can choose to just *adopt the mark* instead. Adopting the mark is as simple as displaying it with the wares when they're sold or advertising your services so that the public understands the mark represents the product. After you have made your first Canadian sale, you have adopted the trademark.

Use is an important concept in trademark law. Using your trademark in Canada establishes your unregistered common-law right to defend it within the geographic area where you're doing business and enjoying a reputation. Advertising your *wares* doesn't count — you must actually make a sale before you can claim your trademark is in use. Advertising your *services,* however, is enough to establish a common-law trademark for them. But remember, the service must actually be available — "coming soon" isn't good enough.

Registered trademarks are indicated by the symbol ®, and marks that have been adopted but not registered can use the symbol ™.

Although adopting a mark is easy, we highly recommend you also take the time to register your mark. Indeed, the best-run companies apply to register trademarks based on *proposed use,* before they actually begin using the mark. Applying based on proposed use lets you define a range of wares and services that you have a bona fide intention of selling in association with your trademark. Applying based on proposed use is more efficient and offers much better potential protection than applying to register the trademark in association with a limited number of wares and services after you've begun selling them.

For example, if you're launching a new soft drink called Chug, you may also plan to sell related merchandise. It's smart to file an application based on the proposed uses of the mark Chug, including uses associated with soft drinks and all sorts of other things you might sell emblazoned with the Chug mark — such as T-shirts, hats, jackets, bags, and golf accessories. In Canada, you must sell each of these items in order for the trademark registration to issue for that item. If you don't use an item on your application within a reasonable time, that part of the application for registration will lapse.

Registering a mark provides you with several advantages, including the following:

 ✓ **The exclusive right to use your mark across Canada.**

 ✓ **An effective legal tool to prevent others from imitating your mark.** Registration provides you with clear ownership, which means that in the event of a legal dispute, the onus of proof will be on the other party — your registered mark is presumed to be valid. If you simply use your trademark, you need to prove entitlement to your rights before you can establish the defendant is violating them — a long, cumbersome process.

 ✓ **Additional value to your business.** A great way to monetize your business is franchising or licensing out your trademark, which is much more easily done with a registered mark (more on licensing in Chapter 7).

Clearing the way

Before adopting or registering the mark, you must *clear* it. This means searching, searching, and still more searching to ensure no one else is using your proposed mark in association with wares or services that are similar or related to the wares and services you propose to sell. The last thing you want is to go to the expense of printing up packaging, labels, and advertisements, only to discover that someone else has beaten you to the punch. A good search can also help you learn more about your competitors and strengthen your mark.

Lexus is a well-known mark associated with cars made by Toyota, and it co-exists with a registration of Lexus used in association with canned tomatoes. This is possible because the wares are very different and the channels of trade for cars and food are very different. Conversely, when an import company applied to register the mark Jaguar in association with luggage, the application was refused because the carmaker Jaguar successfully challenged it. The carmaker had previously made branded luggage available to its customers, and the court decided that luggage is a natural extension of wares associated with the brand.

Hunting for a trademark is a peculiar kind of search because you're actually hoping to not find anything. A similar mark or business name used on similar wares and services or used in a similar channel of trade may cause confusion in the marketplace. Finding such a mark is known as a *knockout*. And it's going to knock you all the way back to the drawing board. Be warned that the probability of a knockout is quite high. It's wise to have a few options to search, because you'll likely go through at least three before you stumble upon one that's available for your use.

Finding registered trademarks

Hiring a qualified trademark searcher who has access to all the relevant databases is the best way to do a trademark search. Your IP professional can order and review a search for you. The cost of the search will depend on how comprehensive it is, but remember that no amount of searching can prove conclusively what is or isn't actually out there.

In Canada, trademark searches start with the Trademark Register in Ottawa. The Canadian Intellectual Property Office (CIPO) maintains the Register, and you can find the database online at www.ic.gc.ca. People on the Trademark Register are serious about their marks. They've gone to the trouble and expense of registration, and they mean business. In all likelihood they have retained a registered trademark agent to help with the application and with monitoring and policing the efforts of others attempting to register a potentially conflicting mark. If you find a mark here that reminds you of your own, you've got potential trouble.

While you're at it, checking out the U.S. trademark site at www.uspto.com is a good idea. Some companies operate in both Canada and the U.S., but go to the expense of registering their trademark only in the U.S. This site will help alert you to any such cases before it's too late.

Seeking out adopted trademarks

If you make it over the first hurdle, and aren't knocked out by any registered marks, it's time to expand your search to adopted but unregistered trademarks.

Checking the Government of Canada name search database (http://nuans.com) is a great next step. The system includes information on corporate names issued federally and by the provinces of British Columbia, Alberta, Ontario, New Brunswick, Nova Scotia, and PEI. You can also search for names and marks that aren't exact matches but that are similar enough to cause confusion to the public (and consternation to you).

Additionally, searching telephone books and business registers will help you to weed out any unregistered names.

Applying for registration

If you choose to follow our advice to register your trademark, you're in for a long but worthwhile journey. The application process can take 12 to 18 months, but after your trademark is registered — and if the registration remains unchallenged — your trademark will be valid for 15 years. Processing your registration is a six-step process:

  ✔ **Formalities:** First you (or your IP professional) fill out an application form, complete with your name and address, a description or drawing of your mark (as appropriate), and a statement indicating details of your first sale in

Canada or your plan to introduce your mark to Canada — including a list of the wares and/or services used, or to be used, in association with your mark. After it's complete, the application form and, of course, your application fee are forwarded to the Trademark Office (TMO). The TMO reviews your application to ensure it's been completed satisfactorily. After the TMO is satisfied your paperwork is in good order, it opens your application file and sends you an application number and filing date.

✔ **Examination:** An examiner at the TMO goes over your application with a fine-toothed comb. And, ideally, he or she confirms that your proposed mark doesn't conflict with any existing ones and that the product or service to be covered is described appropriately. The findings of this stage are sent to you in an official Examiner's Report.

Promptly responding (in writing) to any objections raised in the Examiner's Report will keep your application active.

If you don't convince the examiner to withdraw the objections raised, your application will be rejected — and if you don't respond at all, your application will lapse into abandonment.

✔ **Advertisement:** The TMO publishes applications that successfully pass through the examination stage in the *Trademarks Journal.* This official publication of the Canadian Intellectual Property Office allows third parties, usually other people with marks to protect, to review your mark and register their opposition if they feel it potentially conflicts with their own.

✔ **Opposition:** If your mark meets with opposition, it is removed from the normal processing cycle and placed on hold until the opposition proceedings are complete.

✔ **Allowance:** After your application successfully passes through the process, the TMO issues you a Notice of Allowance and (you guessed it) a request for payment of the registration fee.

✔ **Registration:** After you submit the appropriate fee, your trademark proceeds to registration and you receive an official certificate. This is your proof that you are the registered owner of the mark.

Retaining your registered mark

Like most good things, having a registered trademark comes with some responsibilities. In order to keep the trademark valid, you must

- ✔ **Renew it every 15 years.** So long as you remember to renew it regularly, it'll be yours in perpetuity.

- ✔ **Use it.** The mark must be used for all the wares and services for which it was registered. You have a free ride for the first three years of registration. After that, if you don't use the mark for a period of three years or more, your competitor(s) can apply to have it removed from the register. So, use it or lose it.

  Before and after registration, you must use your trademark in a manner that shows you intend to treat it as a trademark, and not just as text. For example, use a distinctive font or colour when you write it down, so that it stands out from ordinary text, and use the ® symbol (or ™ before it's registered).

  Removing a registered but unused mark is called an _expungement_ under section 45 of the Trade-Marks Act. If your searches turn up a registered mark that is in the way of the one you want to apply for, and it's not being used, you can apply to have the old mark expunged.

- ✔ **Keep it the same.** Your mark should be used in the manner in which it was registered. Companies often make modifications to their mark or logo, but this can cause difficulties with enforcement, because the trademark you are using may not be the same as the one you registered. Consult your IP professional as your company evolves — you may need to reapply with a new mark.

Going international

Acquiring foreign trademark rights is done on a country-by-country basis, and registering your trademark is vital when you're launching a new product or service into a new market where you don't have the benefit of established goodwill. Applying all the principles of searching and establishing good trademark protection is key as you expand abroad.

Centralized filing options

Although in most cases trademarks must be applied for country by country, if you want to register your trademark in three or more European Union/European Community countries, you can take advantage of the Community Trademark System (CTM). The CTM covers all 27 members of the European Union/European Community, and allows you to submit one central application that will be filed in your three (or more) chosen countries, saving you valuable time and money.

The Madrid System for international registration of marks allows centralized applications for all of its 84 member countries. Unfortunately, Canada is not a member, but if you operate an industrial or commercial business in one of the member countries you may be able to take advantage of this system — consult your IP professional.

Filing your first application in association with specific wares or services establishes an *international priority date*. When you file foreign applications in the subsequent six months, you can claim the priority date — your foreign applications will be treated as if they were filed on the same date as your first one. Taking advantage of your priority date allows you to defer the costs of filing foreign applications without compromising the date of adoption. If you don't file internationally within this six-month period you don't automatically lose your right to file, but because you've lost your priority you do run the risk that someone else will file before you.

Trademark applications are prosecuted as a fresh application in each country, and local rules apply. Be aware that many countries are "first to file" jurisdictions, and don't have the examination process that Canada does. This makes it important to establish priority and to get your foreign application on file as quickly as possible.

Canada is unusual because trademark applications here aren't "class-based"; instead, you describe your wares and services in detail. In other countries, the application you file and the filing fee(s) you pay will depend on the number of classes you designate. Be warned that designating many classes will cause costs to rise rapidly!

Enforcing Your Mark

A trademark can be a very valuable asset to your company, and you need to look after it.

You must control the use of your mark. If third parties begin using your mark without your control, then by definition the mark is no longer a signifier that the wares and services originate from you, and it ceases to be a trademark. This means that you must

✔ Prevent third parties from using your mark without authorization,

✔ Clearly control the use of the mark when you authorize a third party to use it, and

✔ Stop third parties from registering marks that are confusingly similar to your mark.

Opposing confusing registrations is essential. Just as third parties had the right to oppose your trademark application, you can (and should) oppose applications by third parties if you believe their mark will create confusion with yours.

If you permit a third party to use your mark, make sure that they adhere to proper licensing standards and that they clearly acknowledge your ownership of the mark and right to control its use. If you mention the trademark of a third party in your advertising (as happens when, say, Future Shop has a sale on iPods), identify the proper owner of the trademark (that is, not you).

As with so many other things in IP law, you must protect the rights to your good name — no one else will do it for you.

Infringing on your rights

Infringement occurs when a competitor uses a mark similar enough to your registered trademark to cause confusion. Whether or not the competitor intended to piggyback on your good reputation, if common sense tells you that your customers (or potential customers) might mistake this product for your own, then infringement has occurred. If you discover someone is using your mark without your permission, you can bring an infringement action against that person or organization and ask the court to put an end to it. Your lawyer has to prove only two things:

> ✔ You're the registered owner of the mark (your certificate of registration will come in handy here), and

> ✔ The mark is confusingly similar to your registered trademark, and is being used without your permission.

After you satisfy both requirements, the court will order the infringer to stop immediately. Depending on circumstances, the bad guys may also be forced to change their name or brand, to destroy current inventory, and/or to pay compensatory damages. See what a powerful tool a registered trademark can be?

Be vigilant about potential infringers, and shut them down quickly. Owners of famous marks, like Harley-Davidson, need to watch the marketplace constantly, taking to task knock-off artists and infringers.

Sometimes, if the marks are not identical, or the wares and services are different, determining infringement can be a judgment call. It's difficult to say with certainty that confusion will arise in the mind of the reasonable consumer. If you have evidence that actual confusion has already occurred, make sure you document it; it'll make your life in court much easier. For example, keep track of any mistaken calls or inquiries you've received that were meant for the other guys. Note any instances that have come to your attention where one of your customers has purchased goods or services from the infringer, thinking she was buying from you.

A related problem that arises with successful trademarks is *genericide*. The public becomes so familiar with a mark that the rights associated with it become diluted. For example, a mark may be used in an inappropriate way, such as being turned into a verb — "Xeroxing" a document instead of photocopying it, or going "Rollerblading" instead of inline skating. Marks may also become so common that they no longer distinguish the product from its competition. For example, people use the phrase Q-Tips for all cotton swabs, regardless of the manufacturer. The same can be said for Escalator, Kleenex, Hoover, Scotch tape, and many, many more.

Some companies believe a high level of generic use is a benefit, as it shows how popular their product has become. Don't fall prey to this assumption — allowing such (mis)use by the public to continue makes it much more difficult to enforce your trademark rights. You don't want the courts to think you have abandoned the mark and allowed it to fall into the public domain.

Passing it off

If you've ignored our advice and haven't registered your trademark, don't despair; you can still defend your rights. Because your mark is unregistered, it's not covered under the trademark statute and therefore you have a smaller set of rights to defend. However, if you think someone is imitating your mark, you can have your lawyer seek relief through the common-law remedy known as *passing off*. This common-law tort prevents others from misrepresenting their products as being associated with yours — that is, it stops them from passing off their products as yours.

Bringing a passing-off action against your competitor is onerous, as your side bears the burden of proof. Your lawyer needs to convince the court that

✔ You have adopted the trademark and enjoy a reputation with the mark.

✔ The third party has been using your mark with the intention of cashing in on your reputation (passing it off as yours).

✔ Damages have occurred as a result of the unauthorized use.

Although the upfront effort of registering your mark may seem like a pain, registration provides you with more robust rights to prevent unauthorized use of your mark. In the event you need to enforce your rights, the burden on you, your business, and your legal team is much less taxing if you've registered.

What's a trademark worth?

All this talk about spending time developing a unique mark, searching out potential conflicts, applying for registration, and defending it against misuse may have you wondering if it's really all worthwhile. It's impossible to pinpoint the exact value of a trademark because each one is unique, but consider this story for a glimpse into how valuable they can be.

Polaroid was famous for its Land cameras that produced instant photos, but in an era of digital cameras the instant print business died and Polaroid went bankrupt twice. Recently, Polaroid's remaining assets — little more than the worldwide trademark rights and associated goodwill — were sold for nearly $100M to a private equity firm that saw enduring value in the name.

Now, we're not saying that registering your mark will lead you to millions; we're simply pointing out that your rights can be quite valuable and they are worth defending.

Chapter 4

Asserting Your Copyrights

* *

In This Chapter

▶ Checking out copyright basics

▶ Understanding ownership

▶ Getting registered

▶ Recognizing infringement

▶ Protecting your rights

▶ Knowing the exceptions

* *

*O*f all the types of intellectual property rights, copyrights are probably the easiest to understand. Certainly they're the easiest to acquire. However, for all its apparent simplicity, the concept of copyright is like a fish underwater: easy to see, but hard to get a grip on — and this is a fish worth grabbing.

In the past, copyrights have been treated like the ugly duckling of IP rights (largely because IP professionals don't make much money helping you acquire or file copyrights). But copyright law is rapidly turning into the swan of IP and is becoming very important for many industries, especially software and entertainment. Whether applied to open source software, downloading and sharing music, video games, or movies, copyrights often determine who can do what — and who makes money. If you intend to create a new ringtone, or simply have someone design a new Web site for your business or charity, you need to understand copyrights. To help you get a handle on copyrights, in this chapter we look at the various kinds of works protected by copyright, who owns these works, and the rights held by the copyright owner.

Working It Out

A *copyright* is primarily an exclusive right allowing the owner of the rights in a qualifying work to prevent others from making copies of the protected work for an extended period of time.

In Canada copyrights generally last for life of author plus 50 years. (In the U.S., it's life of author plus 75 years.) When you consider how little it costs to get the rights in the first place, this makes obtaining copyright protection the single best deal in IP. Conversely, however, it means that if you want to reproduce a work, you need to track down the copyright owner — and you can't assume he won't enforce his rights just because the work is old.

To qualify for copyright, a work must be substantial — copyright isn't available for bumper stickers or titles. Eligible works fit into one of these broad categories:

- ✔ **Literary works:** A written or recorded sequence of words, numbers, or symbols, including books, pamphlets, and computer programs.

- ✔ **Musical works:** Compositions that include music or a combination of music and lyrics (lyrics alone would be covered under literary works).

- ✔ **Dramatic works:** Works that incorporate the spoken word to be performed by one or more characters, including plays, films, scripts, and videos.

- ✔ **Artistic works:** Two- and three-dimensional works of fine, graphic, or applied art, including paintings, photographs, sculptures, maps, and architecture.

Three other categories are eligible for protection, and although they aren't strictly works of authorship, creating them entitles you to prevent unauthorized duplication:

- ✔ A performer's performance
- ✔ A sound recording
- ✔ A communication signal

Open source isn't copyright-free

Many people mistakenly believe that open source software is software without copyrights. However, just because source code is available for free, doesn't mean no copyrights pertain to it.

Normally, copyright to open source software remains with the author, and most open source software is available for use only under licence. The licences often have quite specific (and sometimes onerous) terms. What these licences lack is the obligation to pay a fee. This makes open source licences royalty-free, but not copyright-free.

Whether or not databases of information attract copyright protection has been a contentious issue. For example, can a competitor simply copy and distribute the phone book without the permission of the original creator? On the one hand, the works do not appear to have a scintilla of creativity or original expression. On the other hand, collecting data often requires a significant investment of time and money, and that investment may require protection. The United States has extended broader protection than Canada, but this remains a difficult area — consult an IP professional.

If you write it, they will come

Here's some good news — copyrights come to you automatically. That's right: They arise on authorship of your work. Writing the next book-club bestseller or recording the next chart-topping song? As soon as you do, it's copyrighted.

Just to be clear, though, the bestseller still germinating inside your head isn't covered. A work isn't accepted as existing unless it's been fixed in some form. For instance, if you give a brilliant off-the-cuff speech (without prepared notes) it isn't protected unless you are recording it in some way, perhaps with a stenographer or a video recorder.

Being an original

To be eligible for copyrights, the work must be original. This doesn't necessarily imply that it's new, unusual, or innovative — it simply means that the work is the result of creativity and hasn't been copied from a pre-existing source.

Copyright doesn't protect the *idea* behind your original work; it protects the *original expression* of the idea. For example, taking a photograph of someone else's photograph doesn't qualify as original work. However, if you travel to the same location, look down the same valley, place your camera in the same spot as the original photographer and take your own photo, then you've made an original work.

Untangling Ownership Issues

Generating an original work, whether it's a musical recording, graphic, promotional material, textbook, or photograph, raises ownership and protection issues. Generally, the author of a work is the first owner of the copyright. However, any original creation is potentially valuable, and when money's involved you know things won't remain simple for long.

Creating ownership

If you've been plugging away in your basement and are finally finishing up the next bestseller, the ownership of the manuscript's copyright is likely pretty simple: You're the creator, so you own the copyright. However, paying someone to create a work muddies the waters. Consider the following situations:

- ✔ **Employees' creations:** If you're an employee creating a work as part of your employment, then you don't own copyright, your employer does.

- ✔ **Works created on a for-hire basis:** Hiring someone under contract to provide you with some sort of deliverable creates a stickier situation. Because the person you hire isn't considered an employee, as the original author the copyright will revert to them if you don't specify otherwise. Consider this example: You hire a firm to create some ad copy for you. Although you have freedom to use the agency's materials as per your contract, you don't own copyright to the text or artwork. That means if someone else copies your ads, you can't go after them for infringement — you have to get the advertising agency to pursue them. And, to make things more complicated,

you — not the agency — may own the trademark rights
to the logo in the same ads (see Chapter 3 for information on trademark rights).

Each work-for-hire situation is different, and you can tailor
it to suit your specific needs. For example, you can specify
in the hiring contract that copyright will be assigned to you.
Have a competent IP professional review your contract before
signing to make sure you've protected your rights.

Be aware that anyone contributing to an original work may have
a partial interest in the ownership of that work. Be careful if
you're downloading software from the Net and incorporating it
into your next great application. Other people may be lining up
for payment after it becomes a smash hit. Many costly copyright
litigations involve questions over ownership. The usual partici-
pants in the great ownership debate are associates, employers/
employees, collaborators, and contractors. Consulting an IP professional will help you understand the legalities of ownership.

Joining forces

If you work (on your own, not as an employee) with a co-
author, then you jointly own the copyright, unless you have
an agreement to the contrary. Drafting a *co-ownership agreement* is wise in these cases. Similar to a shareholder agreement, these address many of the issues that may arise in the
future, including derivative uses (such as creating a revised
edition of the work) and succession planning.

Transferring ownership

Determining that you are in fact the owner of the copyright
can open up opportunities for you beyond simply defending
your work from infringers. As the owner, you can license or
assign your work. *Licensing* your work to a third party allows
it to use your work while allowing you to maintain ownership
of the work and copyrights. *Assigning* your work to one, or
more, third parties transfers both the right to use the work
and the copyrights. (See Chapter 7 for details on how to profit
from copyright transfers.)

Entire industries, like movies, music, gaming, and software,
are premised on the licensing of copyrights, so be sure to

have your ownership ducks in a row. If you can't prove that you either own the copyright in a work, or have a licence that permits you to re-license it, then your commercialization of a work will get stopped in its tracks. For businesses that hire contractors and employees to help develop any form of copyrighted work, having clear paperwork that specifies ownership of the copyrights (and any waivers of moral rights) is absolutely crucial. Consult your IP professional.

Making It Official

Registering your work is not necessary in Canada. Because copyrights arise automatically (refer to the previous section for more), pursuing infringers all the way to court is possible without any official certification. You can even mark your work with a © without registering it. However, applying for copyright registration is a quick and easy process, and we recommend that you do so. Arriving at court armed with a certificate of registration makes your life much easier, because the onus of proof will now be on your opponent.

Applying is as easy as completing an application form and sending it to the copyright department at the Canadian Intellectual Property Office (CIPO), along with your application fee, of course. Applying for copyright registration is much easier than applying to register other types of IP. You'll just need to include the title of your work, determine which category it fits into — literary, dramatic, musical, or artistic — note the publication details (date and place of publication) if applicable, and name the author of the work and the owner of the copyright.

Including a copy of the work with your application is not necessary; CIPO will just review your application for completeness. If everything is in order, you'll be hanging your certificate on the wall within a matter of weeks.

If you have several works to protect you need to file separately for each one, because no blanket protection exists.

With any luck, creating and registering your work hasn't left you too tired, because policing your rights is up to you. CIPO registers the copyright and sends you a certificate, but it doesn't enforce your rights. (Check out the next section for more about protecting your copyright.)

Infringing Copyright

Someone is *infringing* on your rights if they do anything that the Copyright Act says only an owner can do. Common violations include copying, performing, importing, or selling a work without authorization from the copyright owner.

The *golden rule* of copyright is simple to define, but it's not always easy to interpret. Copyright doesn't protect the *idea* behind a work. It only protects the *original expression* of the idea. Consider this example:

You write a nifty iPhone application for your employer, and decide to quit your job and write the same application to run on a BlackBerry. No copyright exists in the idea of your application, but copyright does exist in the code, so you must make sure you start entirely from scratch and don't use any of the same code. And remember, if someone in the Ukraine, who has never seen your iPhone application, writes the exact same application from scratch, they're not infringing on your copyright because the idea of the application isn't protected.

Computers and the internet have made copyright infringement a much bigger problem than in the past, and a much easier trap to accidentally fall into.

The fact that you *can* copy something doesn't mean that you *have the right* to copy it.

Consider that the founders of Pirate Bay, a popular Web site for the sharing of music files, were recently sentenced to lengthy prison terms in Sweden for copyright infringement. And, closer to home, the Law Society of Upper Canada (Ontario) was involved in lengthy (read, expensive) litigation that went all the way to the Supreme Court of Canada. The case involved the making of photocopies of case law for lawyers without the permission of the book publishers. So be forewarned that everyone can get into trouble.

Whether you're hunting for photographs to use on your Web site, handing out materials to students in your class, or downloading music to your MP3 player, you need to be attentive to copyright issues. Businesses or institutions that are using copyrighted materials in their products or services must be particularly careful, because copyright owners are more likely to sue an infringer who profits from the infringement. For instance, if your business uses, modifies, or distributes any form of software, you should invest a significant amount of energy into making sure you clear copyright in any software that you bring in or send out.

Reading Your Rights

Being the author of an original work means having some exclusive rights to control how your creation is used, and these extend beyond the right to simply prevent others from copying your work. The following sections discuss the nature and scope of these exclusive rights.

Forbidding copies

The primary and most important right held by the creator or owner of a work, regardless of its category, is to exclude others from duplicating the work. The mere copying is what's forbidden, even if the copy is never used:

- ✔ Copying your own portrait bought from a photographer infringes on the photographer's copyright. The fact that you paid good money for the original and some copies of the portrait doesn't automatically transfer the copyright to you.

- ✔ Downloading a pirated copy of a song or computer program onto your hard drive is committing an act of copyright infringement.

- ✔ Installing or downloading a legitimate copy of software without a licence to do so is considered infringement.

- ✔ Using copyrighted popular music as background for your home video production is a violation of the composer or songwriter's rights.

Prohibiting preparation of derivative works

A *derivative work* arises when a further creative contribution is overlaid onto a pre-existing work. This includes recasting, transforming, or adapting the previous work. Nobody has the right to make a derivative work based on your work without your permission. Here are some examples of derivative works:

- ✔ Translating a book into a different language
- ✔ Creating new lyrics for an old song
- ✔ Photographing a statue
- ✔ Modifying a computer program to make it compatible with a different hardware or software product

Preventing unauthorized distribution

Distributing copies or adaptations of a work, whether by public sale, free distribution, rental, lease, or loan, is an infringement, even if you didn't actually make the copies. For example, copying a clipping from a newspaper or magazine about the impact of secondhand tobacco smoke and giving copies to all your chain-smoking relatives is a no-no. So is passing a copy of a spreadsheet program, licensed only to you, to one of your associates.

Barring public performances

You can prevent the public performance, for profit, of a copyrighted work at a theatre or other place of entertainment.

If you own a copyright on a piece of popular music, you can prevent anyone else from playing a recording of it in public, such as in the background at your favourite martini bar (see Chapter 7 for more information about licences).

A radio or TV station can't broadcast any copyrighted music or video program without a licence from the copyright owner. In Chapter 7, we explain how public broadcasters obtain such licences.

Protecting your artistic reputation

Moral rights are a special brand of copyrights, giving you the ability to maintain credit for your work and protect your reputation. Even if you transfer your copyrights to someone else, moral rights remain with you. This means you can still:

- ✔ Claim authorship of the work.
- ✔ Prevent the work from being associated with a product or cause that's detrimental to your honour or reputation.
- ✔ Stop the modification of your work if it interferes with the integrity of the work.

Canadian artist Michael Snow created a sculpture based on a flock of geese, which were suspended by wires from the ceiling of Toronto's Eaton Centre. Some years later, a decorator decided to place Christmas ribbons around the necks of the geese. The artist objected, claiming that the ribbons interfered with the integrity of his work. The court agreed that his moral rights had been violated, and the ribbons were removed.

You might think that moral rights apply only to the artistic community, and don't concern you as a businessperson. However, consider this scenario. You commission an artist to create a logo for your company and he transfers the copyright to you. Years later, a cigarette company offers to buy your logo for big bucks, but the deal falls apart because the artist refuses to have his work associated with cigarettes.

Although moral rights cannot be transferred to another owner, It's possible to waive them, either in whole or in part. Having your IP professional include a full waiver of moral rights when you arrange the copyright transfer is a good idea.

Exceptions to the Rules

Of course, for every rule an exception exists, and copyrights are no different. Certain activities that would ordinarily infringe on a copyright are allowed in particular circumstances. We discuss some of the common exceptions below, but you should know that the exceptions are narrower in Canada than in other countries. For instance, a parody of an original work is much more likely to be guilty of infringement here than in the United States.

Dealing fairly

The concept of *fair dealing* allows others to use your copyrighted work (published or unpublished) without your permission for the purposes of research or private study. Of course, fairness is one of those subjective criteria about which you and the user of your work may disagree — so the law spells out what's fair use of copyrighted material:

- ✔ Reviews or criticism of the work
- ✔ News reporting
- ✔ Teaching
- ✔ Scholarship
- ✔ Research

Claiming exemptions and privileges

Some activities that would otherwise infringe on a copyright are allowed for specific nonprofit, charitable, or educational purposes.

- ✔ **Copies for the blind:** Literary works may be reproduced or distributed as copies or recordings in specialized formats exclusively for use by blind or other disabled persons. Braille copies of a text or talking books are examples of this type of exemption.

- ✔ **Libraries and archives:** Public libraries, archives, and museums may reproduce and distribute one copy or phonorecord of a copyrighted work for study or research purposes. Copying is also permitted to assist in managing their collections (making a copy for insurance purposes, for example).

- ✔ **Teachers:** Teachers can perform or display a copyrighted work for their students in a face-to-face teaching activity in the classroom of a nonprofit educational institution.

✔ **Ephemeral recordings:** Radio and TV studios may make temporary recordings of their programs for internal use, under certain conditions.

✔ **Personal use:** Finally, an exemption familiar to everybody. You may record a radio or television program while it's played on the air for later listening or viewing by you and the members of your household. You may not, without permission from the copyright owner, copy, sell, lend, or publicly play your recording.

The most important feature of these exceptions is that they are relatively narrow and apply to a relatively small range of acts. Copyrights are routinely violated, either knowingly or unwittingly (see the "Infringing Copyright" section in this chapter), but assuming that you won't get caught is poor business, and pleading ignorance is a poor defence. When in doubt, consult your IP professional.

Chapter 5

Discovering Industrial Designs

In This Chapter

▶ Looking into industrial designs

▶ Navigating the registration process

*W*e know your mother always told you that looks don't matter, but she was wrong. In fact, industrial designs are judged solely on their looks. These IP rights deal with specific visual aspects of a product. And even though industrial designs are lesser known than the other types of IP we discuss in this book, such as patents and copyrights, they can be an effective IP tool.

Designs aren't just a poor man's patent. In fact, we think that design rights are probably the most underutilized of all the IP rights, and in an era when companies like Apple have shown that a growing market exists for well-designed products, we strongly recommend you watch your designs. In this chapter we discuss how registering your designs can help keep you looking good.

Defining Designs

An *industrial design* is a decorative, nonfunctional part of a finished article that you mass produce. It can refer to shape, arrangement, pattern, or decoration — for example, the shape of the arm on a chair, a decorative pattern applied to the product you are selling, or a piece of ornamentation on a set of cutlery. Designs protect just the cosmetic features that are visible to the eye. Only features that are both new and nonessential to the function of the article are eligible for protection.

If you make an original work of art or craft — such as a chair — the design elements are protected by copyright (see Chapter 4). But when you make more than 50 of these "articles," you lose copyright protection in the design. And, if you fail to secure industrial design rights, your design will be open for all to copy.

The range of possible articles that can be protected by industrial designs is very wide, and includes almost anything: car parts, motor boat hulls, shoes, or furniture, to name just a few. Whether your product is sexy, cool, or just plain good looking, you should investigate design rights.

Imagine you've gone to the trouble and expense of launching your great new product and it becomes known for its fabulosity. Consumers recognize the distinctive whatchamacallit on the package and equate it with your superior product. Harried shoppers don't always have time to focus, and they reach for what they recognize on the shelf. A design registration allows you to stop your copycat competitors from putting a similar whatchamacallit on their product and diverting sales that should, rightfully, be yours.

Heading for trouble

When Head & Shoulders debuted, the anti-dandruff shampoo was launched with a substantial advertising campaign. The light green shampoo was packaged in a distinctive bottle with a long neck and sloping shoulders. People quickly came to equate the colour and bottle shape with the good-quality shampoo.

However, soon the shelves were crowded with other green shampoos in strangely similar bottles. Other shampoo manufacturers were hoping to piggyback on the advertising dollars and reputation of the Head & Shoulders shampoo. If the makers of Head & Shoulders had obtained a design registration for the shape of the bottle, the imitators would not have been able to take advantage in this way.

Like most IP rights, industrial design rights are preventive in nature — having them doesn't give you a right to do something specific with your design, and having them doesn't generate sales, but they do give you the right to stop others from manufacturing, selling, or importing an article that incorporates the covered design.

In the United States, industrial designs are called *design patents*. This name highlights the nature of the rights and how you get them, but like all areas of IP, tricky rules exist that vary country by country. So be careful, and use an IP professional with expertise in this specific area.

Registering Your Design

Unlike copyrights (refer to Chapter 4), industrial design rights don't arise upon creation. In Canada, you must register your creation with the Industrial Design Office (a branch of CIPO) in order to exercise your rights. As with patents and trademarks, you must file separately in each country where you want to protect your design rights.

Like patent rights, a novelty requirement for design rights exists. The rules vary greatly from country to country: some countries have a local novelty requirement, some an absolute novelty requirement, and some (like Canada) a system of blended absolute novelty plus a one-year grace period. In the United States, the first-to-invent, one-year grace period applicable to all disclosures rules apply. Your best course of action is to consult your IP professional and file as soon as possible before making your design public.

In contrast to patents, applying for industrial designs is relatively inexpensive. Generally, the applications are much easier to draft and prosecution is not particularly complex — therefore, designs often cost less than trademarks. Budgeting for a cost of $1,000 to $2,500 per application per country is a reasonable estimate.

In Canada, design rights last for 10 years from the date of registration, provided you remember to pay the maintenance fee at the five-year mark. If the maintenance fees are unpaid, your rights lapse (but you do get a six-month grace period, so if the cheque's in the mail, don't panic). Longer protection is available in some other jurisdictions.

The Industrial Design Office registers your design and issues your design certificate, but doesn't police your rights; you must take responsibility for watching your competitors. If you think someone has copied your creation and take action, you can receive compensation only for the prior three years of infringement. Allowing the use of your protected design for more than five years may be considered *acquiescence* — your inaction is taken as consent for the third party to use your design.

After you register your design, mark it with the industrial design symbol — the letter D inside a circle — and the name of the proprietor. Although this isn't a requirement, it's in your best interest. Without the mark, a court can only grant an injunction that forbids the bad guys from using your design on their product in the future; if they establish that they didn't know they were infringing, the courts will excuse their past behaviour. However, if you've taken the time to mark your design, then in addition to banning the bad guys the court may also award you financial compensation for your troubles.

Introducing the basics

Before you leap into applying for registration, keep a few important things in mind:

- ✔ **Your design registration must be new.** You can't take away the freedom of the public to use something that previously existed.

- ✔ **Although the design must be applied to a completed article, it mustn't be involved with the function of the article.** Remember, it's just for show.

- ✔ **Keep quiet about your design.** No time restrictions exist for filing an application, so long as the design has remained private. That means it has never been sold, in Canada or internationally. It also means that it has never been seen by the public. Someone who owes you an obligation of confidence (like your lawyer, an employee, or a contractor who has signed a nondisclosure agreement) isn't considered a member of the public. Be sure to keep track of your disclosures. When it's gone public the clock starts running — and you'd better too, because now you only have 12 months to file in Canada, and even less time in some other countries.

Ensuring you're entitled to apply

As with other IP rights, it's important to get the ownership of the IP correct. If you hire employees or contractors to design products for you, make sure your business gets a clear assignment of the IP rights in the design.

Canadian design rights are unique because the proper party — the owner of the design, *not* the design's creator — has to apply for registration. Usually a design's proprietor is the creator, although the design can be assigned to someone else, who becomes the proprietor.

Be sure the proprietor files for the design registration. If an application is granted based on misinformation (such as an incorrectly named proprietor), the registration becomes invalid and can't be corrected.

Particular care should be taken when a design has been created by

- ✔ **An employee:** In this case, even though the author is the employee, the employer remains the proprietor, because he mandated and paid for the creation of the design. The employer must apply for registration.

- ✔ **A group of people:** If several people collaborate on a design, then they should all apply as joint proprietors, unless they're working as a team for an employer — in which case the employer applies as a single applicant.

- ✔ **Two companies working together:** They should file jointly as co-applicants.

- ✔ **An outside contractor:** The person who paid for the work should file. But it's best to get a clear assignment of all rights — in writing — just to be safe.

Completing the application

After you establish the correct person to apply for the industrial design registration, you need to get to work on your application. In this section, we give you an overview of an application and the process, but we encourage you to consult an IP professional to assist you with both drafting and following up on your filing. A strong focus on the nitty gritty details and a thorough knowledge of the rules and regulations can make a patent agent a wise investment.

When identifying the design, give some thought to what you want to protect. You can choose to protect just a portion of the article (the shape of the back of a chair) or the whole thing (the shape of a kettle). The scope of what you choose to protect is a delicate balancing act, because if you make your description too wide your design may become impossible to enforce, and if you make it too detailed or specific you may make it easy for someone to evade your design. (See why hiring an IP pro, who can advise you on what to describe, is a good idea?)

Title

You need to give your application a title. Your title should be concise and should identify the article to which you've applied the design — for example, "set of cutlery." Your title's important, because it determines the scope of protection you'll receive. No protection is offered if the same design is applied to a different article, so make sure to identify the complete finished article and not simply one of its component parts.

Description

In your application, you need to describe the article to which you've applied the design and the features that make up the design. Clarity is key. Identify the features and their placement on the article, but make sure you keep the focus on the visual elements only. Don't get carried away with details about how the article was made or how it works. Industrial designs are very superficial; they're all about the looks.

Drawings

The application needs to be supported by at least one visual depiction of the design. Either a photo or a drawing is acceptable, but whichever you choose, the image must be clear and accurate. Drawings are preferable, and a skilled draftsperson should prepare them.

If you end up in court, the judge will use the visual aid you included in your industrial design registration application to determine the outcome of your case.

You can include as many pictures as you believe are necessary to fully show your design, but if the Industrial Design Office feels you have included too many it will ask you to remove the extraneous ones (the IDO doesn't want you to cluttering up its register). Six is a good number that allows you to provide front, back, top, bottom, right-side, and left-side views of your design.

Processing your application

After you sweat over your application, making sure all the *t*'s are crossed and the *i*'s are dotted, it's time to sit back and wait. Your application goes through a six-step process on its way to approval:

1. **Initial processing:** An examiner from the Industrial Design Office reviews your application to ensure you've adhered to all the administrivia. He or she checks to see that you've filled out the forms correctly and that all the requirements (including fee payments) have been met.

   If so, good for you! The Industrial Design Office issues you a *filing certificate* for your troubles. But don't get too excited — this simply means that your application was received in good order, that it will be processed, and that you have an official filing date. It doesn't mean you're certified, yet.

2. **Classification:** Next the IDO will classify your application according to the specific article to which you've applied it (for example, cutlery or chair).

3. **Preliminary examination:** During this stage, an examiner reviews all your paperwork and makes sure your description and drawings provide a clear enough picture for a search to take place.

4. **Search:** An examiner searches out designs that are already published and/or registered — both at CIPO in Canada and elsewhere, typically the USPTO — and compares them with yours. He or she notes any similarities for later review.

5. **Examination:** Don't worry, this won't hurt a bit. An examiner reviews your application and the search results to ensure your design is unique and that you've complied with all the rules and regulations.

   If you pass the exam, congratulations: Your application will be registered. If you fail, don't despair. You can always try again. The examiner will send you a report and explain what additional information is required or what changes you need to make in order to be successful.

6. **Registration:** The finish line! After your application is approved, it's registered and you receive a certificate to prove it.

Jumping the queue

Getting your industrial design reviewed, approved, and registered is not a quick process. All this processing, searching, and examining takes time. In fact, granting design certification will take months (a bare minimum of six, usually closer to a year). However, in some cases timing becomes a critical issue. For instance, if your archrival has already begun to imitate your design, you will want to have your certificate issued ASAP so you can slap an injunction against him. In a case like this, you should file for *priority status,* based on the alleged infringement that's already taking place. Achieving priority status moves you much closer to the front of the line, but be aware that you'll have to pay an additional fee to get on the fast track. In cases like these, the examination begins as soon as you submit the request for accelerated examination.

Life after industrial designs

After your industrial design rights expire, all is not lost. If customers have come to associate the design of your product or packaging with your company as the source of these goods, then you may be eligible to apply for distinguishing guise trademark protection. This is the form of protection used to protect famous packaging designs like the curvy Coke bottle.

And what if your foe has the nerve not only to duplicate your design, but also to file a request to register it? Well, then timing becomes critical. You need to make sure you were first in line. If you've already filed a request to register in another country, then you're in luck — you can use the benefit of *foreign priority*. You can use the date of your foreign filing as your starting point, so long as your Canadian application begins within six months of the foreign one. You must request foreign priority at the beginning of your filing process in Canada. Because industrial designs are processed on a first-come, first-served basis, this option could be vital to your success.

Going international

The Paris Convention is an IP treaty with almost 200 member countries (see Chapter 2 for more details). Although no specific Paris Convention process exists for designs, applicants who live in member countries are able to claim a right of priority (of up to six months) based on their first filing date when they're filing for protection in another member country. For example, if you file in Canada now, you have up to six months to file in the United States. However, because of the absolute novelty requirements in many other countries, if you hope to protect your design outside Canada and the U.S. you must ensure your first filing is made before any public disclosure (no 12-month grace period exists), and you must file the international application within six months of the Canadian application.

Part II
Profiting from Intellectual Property

BOWIE SPATULAS
BOWIE EGG BEATER
BOWIE PUNCH LADLE
BOWIE OLIVE FORK

"I still like his knives the best."

In this part . . .

*P*rotecting your IP from imitators is important, and in this part we explain how you can do this. But fending off copycats is only one benefit of IP. You can also profit from IP by renting or selling your IP rights to generate cash flow. We show you how it's done. We also give you tips on using other people's IP to your advantage — all without infringing on their rights, naturally.

Chapter 6

Enforcing Your IP Rights

*F*rom a legal point of view, your patent, copyright, trademark, or industrial design gives you permission to control who uses your intellectual property. But this permission has many limits and restrictions. You can't just put the meddler under citizen's arrest or seize any counterfeit merchandise; instead, enforcing your rights involves time, money, and lawyers. In this chapter, our goal is to explain some of the procedures particular to IP litigation and point you toward the most expeditious and least expensive approaches.

Catching the Copycats

Determining whether your IP right has been violated requires careful legal analysis of all circumstances. Here we introduce some common infringement issues that you may run into.

Violating copyright

Your copyright can be infringed upon by any of the following methods:

✔ Copying or adapting the protected work

✔ Distributing or displaying copies or adaptations of the protected work

✔ Publically performing a musical or dramatic work

✔ Transmitting the work

Determining whether your copyright's been violated

Some forms of copyright infringement are straightforward and easy to detect. Either a recording of your song aired on the radio, or it didn't. Your paper got published, or it didn't. Period. However, determining infringement isn't always so easy. Say you wrote articles on a freelance basis years ago, and now the newspaper that bought them wants to put the old articles online. Does the newspaper have a right to do something neither side even considered when the articles were first purchased?

Many of the most contentious issues in copyright law involve the role of intermediaries who operate between the copyright owner and a blatant infringer. For example, is an internet service provider liable for illegal downloading by a subscriber? Or consider illegal uploading or file sharing — is someone who hosts a directory of files available for illegal sharing, like Pirate Bay, liable for copyright infringement? Is this different from a search engine that makes it possible to find illegal files?

Knowing whether or not your copyright's been violated requires a little bit of analysis. We summarize the infringement test in four words: access, expression, and substantial similarity. If you suspect infringement, ask yourself these questions:

✔ Did the alleged infringer have access to my work?

✔ Does part of my work constitute a protected expression rather than a pure idea or material already in the public domain?

✔ If I've answered yes to the preceding questions, do the similarities between the part of my work containing the protected expression and the infringer's work indicate that partial or whole copying occurred?

Finally, make certain that the suspected infringement doesn't fall under the fair dealing rules, or one of the copyright exemptions. (Refer to Chapter 4 for a partial listing.)

In most cases, IP owners (or the appropriate licensee) are responsible for enforcing their rights through civil remedies. However, many forms of copyright infringement are considered criminal offences in much of the world. This means that in many countries the state may help you pursue the infringers. Canada's relative lack of criminal sanctions for copyright enforcement is an anomaly and rapidly becoming a major irritant to our trading partners, especially the United States.

Taking a trademark

To determine whether your trademark rights are being violated, you and your legal team must assess whether a likelihood of confusion exists between your trademark and the alleged infringer's. Keep in mind that *likelihood* doesn't mean possibility, it means probability. There needs to be a reasonable expectation that the public will be confused.

Proving the likelihood of confusion in court can be a challenge, because it's really a judgment call. Giving your lawyer proof that actual confusion has already occurred will help your case. Be sure to document any instances that come to your attention. These cases often involve complex survey evidence, which can be expensive to obtain and to attack.

Running afoul of a patent

Proving patent infringement is a costly and complex process, requiring expert legal analysis. We don't expect you to get into the nitty gritty details — after all, that's what you pay your IP professional for.

The bad guys are infringing on your patent only if their device or process includes *all* of the elements listed in any one of your patent claims. Refer to Chapter 2 for our advice on drafting an effective claim.

Infringing on an industrial design

Enforcing your industrial design rights is similar to enforcing both a patent and a trademark. First you must establish that the infringer copied your design, and then you must defend your registration as the infringer tries to establish that it doesn't cover its activity (or, as below, that your registration is invalid).

Pursuing the Infringers

You've done your homework. You're certain that your competitor is selling a bike that includes a pedal-activated whistle, contrary to your patent. What now? First up is a trip to your lawyer. You need an IP professional who is a litigator to help you. Your business lawyer may be willing to help, and so may your patent agent, but it's unlikely that either has the IP and litigation expertise necessary for these complex cases. (Consult Chapter 1 for advice on how to find a good IP pro.) Just as you acquire IP rights country-by-country, you must enforce them country-by-country — so if someone is infringing your copyright in Brazil, likely you need a Brazilian IP pro to go after them.

Firing a warning shot

Instead of heading directly to court, first have your lawyer send the bad guys a stern *cease and desist letter*. This letter advises them that you believe they are infringing on your rights, and demands an immediate stop to all acts of infringement.

Ideally, your lawyer should end the letter with a request for an explanation and an offer of a meeting. After all, your key objective is to have the infringer stop, not to endure the time and financial costs of a lawsuit. It pays to be reasonable.

Meeting with the other side can be very beneficial. For example, is it possible that you're wrong about the violation? Talking with your competitor helps you gain valuable insight even if you are correct about the infringement. For example:

✔ Are they dug in and refusing to comply with your IP rights?

✔ Do they seem the type to fight rather than admit they are wrong?

✔ Do they seem amenable to some sort of compromise?

Even after you've proceeded to court, always remain open to meeting with the opposition. You may be surprised how perspectives change with the passage of time and the payment of mounting legal fees.

Be aware that trials can go on for weeks, and are exceptionally expensive. Cases that involve experts cost well into the hundreds of thousands of dollars, and sometimes more. Take every opportunity to settle. Keep in mind the case of Waterloo-based Research In Motion, which lost a patent case in the U.S. to the tune of $615 million. At the beginning of the case they had the chance to settle for a very small amount. It's not only the settlement costs that add up, but also the diversion of management time and energy, which could be much better spent driving your business. In most situations, the sensible approach to resolving an infringement issue is skillful negotiation.

Proceeding to court

If you're unable to reach an out-of-court settlement with your infringer, your lawyer will initiate court proceedings.

When you get to court, the *burden of proof* — who must prove what — often affects who wins and who loses. Keep in mind that registering your copyrights and trademarks, although optional, provides you with a big advantage — your rights are presumed to be valid. Your opponents bear the burden of proving that your rights should be invalidated. Unregistered rights can be defended, but you must first prove you're entitled to the rights, which complicates and lengthens your trial.

You begin your journey to trial by exchanging *pleadings* with the opposing side; as the plaintiff you declare your claim against the defendant, and the defendant states his defence. Then the parties exchange all relevant documentation — and we do mean *all* relevant documentation. Providing full disclosure is essential, even if some of the papers hurt your case. Should relevant papers disappear, it will count heavily against you. Next, a representative from each side answers questions, under oath, during a pre-trial discovery examination. Finally, it's on to court, which we cover in the section "Fighting for Your Rights."

IP trials often involve highly complex subject matter. In some patent cases, educating the judge about the technology takes up the first days of the trial. Providing an expert witness who understands the subject matter and who presents your version of events is your responsibility. Your legal team will help you secure a qualified candidate, but you'll have to pay the expert's fees. Your opponent will provide his own expert witness and perspective on the events.

Fighting for Your Rights

After you arrive in court, the defendant is entitled to use any of a number of defences recognized by the law. We introduce you to a few of the major ones below.

Questioning the scope of your rights

Your opponent claims that he isn't infringing, because your protection isn't broad enough to cover what he's doing. His actions exceed the *scope of your rights*.

Patents

You define the exclusive rights that will be protected when you draft your claim. Within the claim, you create a list of the innovations for which you are seeking protection. In court, the judge checks the alleged infringements against the list in your claim, and if you include something on your claim that your opponent has omitted, they're not guilty of infringement. (Refer to Chapter 2 for advice on drafting an effective claim.) For example, if your patent claims a whistle fastened to the front wheel of a bicycle, and your opponent fastens his whistle to the back wheel, you have no case. His use doesn't fall within the scope of your claim.

Industrial designs

Submitting a drawing that depicts the look of your product defines your exclusive design rights, and selecting the title of your registration defines the type of product you're protecting. If you choose "bottle" as your title and the infringer is using a similar design on a lamp, that falls outside the scope of your rights. (Chapter 5 has more details on design registration.)

Copyright

Violating a copyright involves copying; coming up with a similar creation independently doesn't count as infringement. Proving to the court that copying has occurred is your responsibility. The court makes a judgment call based on the balance of probabilities — is it more or less likely that copying occurred? If copying didn't occur, then the creation exists beyond the scope of your copyright.

Generally, providing proof that the opposition had access to your work and that a similarity exists between the works will cause the court to rule in your favour.

Trademarks

If the copycat uses your exact trademark on the same type of product you sell, then the case is fairly clear cut and is unlikely to go to court. However, if the marks are merely similar to yours and the wares are slightly different, you need to prove that customer confusion over whose product is whose is likely to arise. If confusion is unlikely, then you can't prevent the use of your trademark.

Invalidating your claim

The bad guys may try to claim that your right is invalid. If they can prove that you aren't in fact entitled to the rights you are defending, the rights will be ruled invalid. Invalidity arguments are usually asserted by way of a counterclaim in response to your claim. If the invalidity claim is successful, this can end your IP rights — which can be a disaster for you and your licensees. In Chapters 2–5 we discuss the requirements you must meet to secure valid IP rights — and you can rest assured that a defendant will probe each possible requirement to challenge the validity of your rights.

Questioning the ownership of your IP

Proving you own your IP right may be necessary, particularly if you acquire the rights through an assignment or transfer. For your own protection, set everything in writing. Registering the transfer of rights with the Canadian Intellectual Property Office (CIPO) isn't a requirement, but it's in your best interest. For example, in the case of a disputed patent (perhaps the original owner sold the patent twice), the first to register wins. Instead of twisting your ankle racing to the patent office at the first sign of trouble, register as soon as the transfer takes place.

Exhausting your rights

Defendants commonly claim you gave them permission, and if it's true, it's a pretty good defence. If the infringer buys whistles from one of your distributors who's going bankrupt — and they really are your whistles — you can't complain. Selling something gives the buyer the implied right of use; your rights become exhausted by the sale. You've used them up and can't assert them a second time.

Claiming you failed to act promptly

Sitting on your IP rights and then leaping out of the bushes to sue an infringer isn't allowed. Knowing about infringement and failing to act is called *acquiescence*. Your opponent may claim that he believed you had waived your rights because you had already been allowing the use of your right for a period of time.

Getting to the Finish Line

Although visions of multi-million dollar settlements may dance in your head when you think of court cases, remember that your main goal when bringing an IP infringement case to court is simply to end the infringement. Reaching the end of an IP case allows you to breathe a little easier. In this section, we consider some of the other potential outcomes of an IP case.

Settlements

Settling is the best, fastest, and least expensive way to end an infringement dispute. Aim to settle if it's at all possible. Here are a couple possible settlements:

- ✓ You and the infringer negotiate a compromise where he continues to use your right on an ongoing basis, in exchange for making payments to you.

- ✓ The infringer agrees to pay you a fee for permission to continue using your right until his existing inventory is cleared out. He will then stop the infringing activity.

Rulings

If you're unable to reach a settlement, the court will make a ruling based on the information presented at trial. A few possible outcomes include the following:

- ✓ **The court issues an *injunction:*** This is an order directing the defendant to stop selling the infringing article. Usually the court also orders that existing inventory be delivered to the holder of the IP right or destroyed. Injunctions can be either *interlocutory* (before the trial) or permanent. In the RIM vs. NTP litigation, the possibility that the court might grant an injunction that shut down all BlackBerry service in the U.S. was front-page news.

- ✓ **You may receive a pay-over of the profits arising from the infringing activities.** Doing so means that you are, legally, condoning the activities, therefore no injunction would be granted.

- ✓ **The court may award you compensation for damages.** You could receive an amount comparable to lost profits or a royalty, reasonable for the amount of infringement that took place.

Chapter 7

Cashing In on Your IP Rights

*I*P rights offer much more value than simply allowing you to prevent copycats from using your creations. Sure, selling the product that embodies your IP right is a good start, but other opportunities to monetize your IP also exist. Always develop your IP assets with an eye toward letting these assets, and your IP rights to them, work like a lucrative investment. You can profit from your IP rights just like you can with a good investment in real estate — you can sell them after they go up in value, retain ownership and collect the royalties they generate (similar to rent), or both.

That dream is a reality for many astute entrepreneurs who took advantage of the opportunities that rewarded their creativity. In this chapter we suggest some of the different ways you can maximize the benefit of your IP.

Selling and Licensing

Commercializing your IP — getting people to pay for it, whether by selling the IP or licensing it — can be quite different from selling your product or service. However, commercializing IP has some real similarities to other business activity: it requires preparation, persistence, marketing, and selling.

IP doesn't commercialize itself. It must be sold, and every ad you've ever seen for a Microsoft product proves this. Not all IP is valuable. Only IP that provides a right to exclude others from doing something that they want to do, and can't get around quickly and cheaply, is valuable. People buy or license IP because it's cheaper and easier to buy or license it than to develop an alternative in-house. For example, if you use Microsoft Word, you likely do so because buying a licence is cheaper and easier than writing your own word processing program.

Most successful IP rights sales depend on the buyer having easier and quicker access to customers than the seller. You may have a great idea for a computer networking device, but chances are Cisco is going to be able to take it to a bigger market faster and with more marketing muscle than you can. If Cisco buys your IP, it steps into your shoes, and can use the IP to protect its product. For the same reason, most successful IP licensing involves vastly expanding the use of the IP through distribution channels that the original creator can't reach directly as easily as the licensee(s) can.

Commercializing IP successfully requires you to adjust your thinking, because IP isn't like tangible property. IP can have

- ✔ **More than one owner.** Although co-ownership can be complex, it can also solve many thorny problems.

- ✔ **More than one simultaneous user,** and can increase in value the more it's used. IP doesn't wear out, and costs nothing to ship.

- ✔ **More than one exclusive licensee,** if the licensees are in different markets.

Here's an example. You're in charge of fundraising for a major university. Chances are, your trademark is one of your most valuable assets, and if you proceed carefully you can license it to more than one third party in exchange for valuable revenue that enhances your brand: affinity credit cards, insurance services, travel packages for seniors, and so on. Many universities are already exploring precisely this sort of trademark licensing strategy as a fundraising tool.

Understanding Licences

Your driver's licence gives you the permission to do something that you previously couldn't — take your car out for a spin on the highway. The government, which owns the highway, gives you this permission as part of a deal. For your licence to remain in effect, you have to uphold your end of the deal: drive responsibly and follow the rules of the road — otherwise they'll take your licence away. An IP licence follows the same principle.

A *licence* is a contract between two parties. The *licensor* owns an IP right. The *licensee* is an individual or company willing to use the IP right in exchange for paying royalties or other valuable considerations. For example, if the IP right is a patent, the licensee can practise the invention without being sued for infringement by the patent-owning licensor.

A licence doesn't actually transfer the IP right — it just gives the licensee permission to use the IP, backed by the licensor's promise not to cancel that authorization as long as the licensee keeps up her end of the bargain. A licence is like the lease on a house, where the landlord gives the tenant permission to live there as long as he pays the rent on time. A licence differs from an *assignment,* which is an outright transfer of an IP right, similar to selling a house. (See "Assigning Rather Than Licensing" in this chapter.)

Granting Licences

Because all IP can be licensed, many different types of licences exist. To get you thinking about the possibilities, we list a few of the common ones below, according to the type of underlying IP right:

✔ **Patent licence:** You can license your patent rights, whatever they may be, as soon as they arise. That means you can license them from the time of invention — before any patent is granted — and benefits of this can include having the licensee assume the costs of prosecuting and maintaining the patent in its territory. In situations such as these, consider who enforces the patent, and what the consequences will be if the patent is deemed partially or wholly invalid.

✔ **Trade-secret licence:** The licensor discloses proprietary and confidential information to the licensee in exchange for payment and a promise to keep the information under wraps. Trade secret licences are particularly common in the chemical field, where keeping formulae and manufacturing processes secret is relatively easy.

✔ **Copyright licence:** A copyright licence allows the licensee to use the copyrighted work. Often these licences are named for their use — such as a publication licence, broadcast licence, or recording licence. Technically, you don't buy software or ringtones — you buy a licence to use the software or ringtone, and the scope of what you're allowed to do with it is set by the precise terms of the licence.

Registering your copyright before granting a licence isn't a prerequisite, but we highly recommended doing so. Registered rights are much easier to enforce, making the terms of a licence easier to enforce. Additionally, a registered copyright offers better protection against third-party infringers, making it more attractive to licensees, and more valuable to you.

✔ **Trademark licence:** This licence authorizes someone else to operate under one or more of your commercial identifiers. The law requires you to keep some quality control over the activities of your licensee so that the customers who relied on the quality of your goods or services in the past will not be deceived into buying substandard products.

Nowadays, many products aren't made by their original manufacturers but by firms that use the trademark under licence from the original manufacturer and strict quality control conditions. A Mountain Equipment Co-op jacket likely isn't manufactured by employees of the Co-op.

✔ **Merchandising licence:** Certain marks are so strong, recognized, and widely accepted that they can be rented out for use on a wide variety of goods. Merchandising licences allow the use of a copyright or trademark, or a combination of both, on a range of goods that goes beyond the original purpose of the mark. For instance, a movie studio may license the use of a cartoon character on a variety of children's products, from toys to book bags.

Licensing lingo

Here are some terms you should be familiar with if you want to license your IP:

✔ Licences, especially of software, often flow through a chain of licensees. The final customer is usually called the *end user*, and the intermediaries are referred to as *channel partners*. The channel partners are granted a licence to sub-license, but not a licence to use, which is granted only to the end user.

✔ A *value-added re-seller* (VAR) pays you for a licence and then re-sells the licence with a mark-up. A *value-added distributor* (VAD) arranges for a customer to pay the licensor directly for the licence, and the licensor remits the VAD's share to the VAD.

✔ An *original equipment manufacturer* (OEM) is an industrial big

dog — think of the giant carmakers. Licensees often try to license their IP to OEMs, which then incorporate it into their products. This is often easier than trying to sell an after-market product to customize the OEM's product. Windshield-wiper delays are a good example of a product that has transitioned successfully from the after-market to the OEM market.

✔ Permitting a licensee to apply their trademarks on a product or service so it appears to originate from the licensee, not the licensor, is known as *white-labelling*. Chances are the Webmail product that you access from your internet service provider is a white-labelled product licensed from a third-party software developer.

✔ **Franchising:** A franchise is a trademark licence coupled with a noncompetition agreement, and includes rules about how the franchisee will conduct the business according to the method imposed by the franchisor. This type of contractual relationship includes some transfer of know-how and technical assistance by the franchisor (coupled with a hefty down payment by the franchisee). Fast-food franchises are a familiar example, where a franchisee acquires a restaurant carrying the franchisor's name and logo, and prepares and serves food under a set method and strict quality control.

Inspecting the Basic Elements of a Licence

In this section, we highlight the key issues you should address when exploiting your IP assets, and offer some actual text that you can use in legal documents and other legal observations. (That text appears in italics.)

This outline of the basic make-up of a licence agreement isn't exhaustive; seeking the assistance of a competent IP professional to negotiate and draft the licence agreement is a must.

Getting it in writing

Before negotiating any type of licence agreement, you should understand the important parts of the agreement. Here are some key things that you and your lawyer need to cover in the agreement:

✔ **Clearly define the IP right you're licensing.**

✔ **Grant permission to use your IP.** This is a critical part of the licence agreement, because here you define the scope of the permitted activities. Be very specific here in order to avoid future disputes.

✔ **Determine the level of exclusivity** — who gets to use the rights.

   • **Exclusive:** The licensor waives any right to use the rights or to authorize anybody else to do so.

- **Sole:** The licensor reserves the right to use the rights himself or through his company, but agrees to license only the licensee.

- **Non-exclusive:** The licensor reserves the right to use the rights and can also license third parties in competition with the licensee.

In general, an exclusive licence carries higher royalties than the other two types.

✔ **Outline the territory and field of use.** An IP owner can divide and parcel the geographical areas and commercial fields where the invention can be practised or applied.

For example, say you hold a patent on energy-efficient window frames. Because they're reasonably priced and work well, you sell a number of them. You'd like to expand your territory and sell more, but because windows are heavy and fragile, they don't travel well. Licensing your patent to window makers in other markets is a perfect option for this situation; you can continue to service your home territory, while your licensees pay you royalties to use your invention in theirs.

✔ **Define the duration.** Fix the term of the licence and any renewals, and deal with what happens if the IP right is lost or is no longer enforceable against third parties.

✔ **Address enforcement.** Determine who has what rights and obligations to enforce the IP and to shut down infringers. It's no fun paying a royalty to the licensor if your competitor is using the IP for free.

✔ **Specify termination.** State when the licence can be terminated, and what happens if it is. Software licences often require the licensor to place the source code in escrow, for release to the licensee in certain circumstances. If you are the licensee of any IP right, protecting yourself against arbitrary termination if the licensor goes bankrupt is very important and, in light of the current state of the law in Canada, very difficult, even for the most experienced IP professionals.

If the licence authorizes the licensee to use or operate under your trademark, include a clause allowing you to control the quality of the goods or services provided to the customer under your identifier. This allows you to maintain quality and service standards, and therefore the value of your trademark.

Getting paid: Remuneration

You have great flexibility when setting up the payment for the licence. Payments may comprise

✔ One or more lump sums

✔ Royalties based on net proceeds, number of items made or sold, costs of goods, or any other readily verifiable parameter

✔ A combination of the above

Advances against royalties, delayed payments, stepped-up or stepped-down royalty rates based on sale proceeds or number of items sold, and guaranteed remittances can be used to fine-tune the agreement to your circumstances:

> *Licensee shall pay Licensor each of the following:*
>
> *A non-refundable lump sum of $5,000.00 on each anniversary of the effective date of this agreement.*
>
> *During the first 10 years of the term of this agreement, royalties at the rate of $10.00 per camera manufactured under the exclusive and co-exclusive licences, and at the rate of $3.00 per camera manufactured under the non-exclusive licence; plus 1% of the net proceeds from the sales of all types of cameras. After the 10th anniversary of the effective date of this agreement, these royalty rates shall be reduced by one half.*
>
> *A royalty advance of $25,000.00 upon execution of this agreement by all parties.*

The details of the remuneration clause are usually dictated by the business circumstances — the financial status and marketing clout of the licensor, the anticipated sales, the required investment in tooling and marketing, and so on.

Think carefully about what the royalty is applied to. If you charge the licensee a royalty as a percentage of revenue from one product, but it also sells to the same customers another product or service that isn't under licence, the licensee has an incentive to under-price your product and mark up the other service.

Including a minimum performance clause with an exclusive licence agreement is wise because you depend entirely upon the licensee's performance to exploit your IP asset. Such a clause may use a sliding scale to keep the licensed company on its best behaviour. For example:

> *Licensee shall pay Licensor:*
>
> *In the first calendar year, $50,000.00,*
>
> *In each subsequent year, the greater of $150,000.00 or one half of the total monetary remuneration received by licensor during that year.*

Reporting

Except when licence fees are fully paid upfront or by a fixed payment schedule, requiring the licensee to periodically report its production and/or sales figures is smart, as royalties are based on these numbers:

> *Within thirty days from the end of each calendar year, Licensee shall provide Licensor with a report of the number of cameras manufactured and net proceeds collected by Licensee during that calendar year.*

Assigning Rather Than Licensing

When IP is transferred outright, whether from employee to employer, or from company to company, it's done using a written document called an *assignment.*

When your lawyer drafts the assignment document, make sure she includes a complete and readily identifiable description of what's being transferred (attach a copy or photograph if necessary). And if the buyer is paying you a royalty rather than a lump sum payment up front, also include in the agreement all the payment and reporting clauses usually found in a licence agreement. (See the "Inspecting the Basic Elements of a Licence" section in this chapter.)

If you're buying the assignment of rights, record the assignment as soon as possible in the Canadian Intellectual Property Office (CIPO), or any other appropriate agency. In general, recording the transfer cuts off the transferor's right to assign the same asset or right to another person. If you don't record the assignment, any subsequent assignment takes precedence over yours if it's recorded first.

Developing a Commercialization Strategy

Many inventors and other developers of IP assets and rights don't have a clue about how to find a buyer or licensee to bring their creations to the market. No magic formula will work for everybody, but planning your commercialization strategy before you pursue IP rights is the best way. Don't panic if you haven't; all is not lost. As long as you understand the marketplace, you can develop an effective and lucrative strategy.

Understanding market realities is the first step to a good commercialization strategy. To help you begin your planning, we offer a few observations based on many years serving entrepreneurs:

- ✔ **The more you develop your project, the more you get for it.** You generally can't sell an idea or concept. A patented but unproven invention may sometimes be sold or licensed, but not for much. If you can show that you have an ongoing business with real customers, built around a product, process, or method protected by IP rights, it can be sold more readily and lucratively than the same business without IP rights.

- ✔ **Few large companies respond to an unsolicited licence offer or proposal.**

- ✔ **The most promising buyers and licensees are companies that can increase their existing sales by owning/ licensing a little of your IP,** especially if they're trying to catch up with a market leader and can use your IP to give them a new edge. For example, a company that sells furnaces may want to buy your latest and greatest internet-enabled thermostat to gain market share in the furnace business. They might even give the thermostat away for free to furnace buyers.

Another very attractive potential group of licensees are people who do what you do, but for a different market. Say you sell diagnostic tools to Canadian dentists. Potential licensees of some of your IP include people who sell diagnostic tools to dentists in other countries, or perhaps veterinarians in Canada and elsewhere.

✔ **Commercialize your IP early, often, and aggressively.** Start commercializing as quickly as you can and don't wait for the IP to be formally granted. This gains you customers, and with customers come revenue and feedback. Revenue keeps you in business, and feedback leads to further improvements. Don't keep your IP in the dark — it grows better in the light of day.

Getting sophisticated help to design and roll out an IP commercialization strategy isn't easy. Most IP professionals are not business experts, and many businesspeople are not IP experts. This leaves a void of people who speak both languages; this book is our small attempt to start a dialogue across this void.

Chapter 8

Benefitting from Someone Else's IP

*I*P provides benefits not only to its owners, but also to outsiders — especially licensees, who can acquire new products, processes, materials, and brands much more efficiently through the use of licences than by developing them from scratch.

Licensing used to be an exotic way to conduct business, but it's rapidly becoming mainstream. The key to successful licensing is to ensure that it's win-win: both the licensor and licensee must gain, both likely contributing something the other doesn't have or can't easily reproduce. In this chapter we consider some of the key benefits of licensing IP into your organization. (For more about the basics of licensing and being a licensor, consult Chapter 7.)

Being a Licensee

If you've ever bought software, you've benefited from licensing someone else's IP. For example, accounting software offers specific applications for all sorts of different markets, such as lawyers, dentists, municipal governments, and so on. To gain access to a high-quality solution at a reasonable cost, users license these applications rather than building them from scratch. This also provides them the assurance that the costs of supporting and maintaining the product will be spread over many users.

Acquiring an exclusive right to use or distribute someone else's IP in your market can give you a substantial boost. Say you're already in the business of selling products and services to pig farmers in Manitoba, and you've heard about ways to cut down on methane emissions while generating electricity and heat from pig manure. Many alternative energy technologies are far more advanced in Europe than they are in Canada. As a result, a possible strategy is to approach European companies that have good technology. Chances are good they don't consider Canada their biggest or most important market (they may not have even considered Manitoba), and they may license their world-leading technology to you for modest royalties. If they do, this will quickly and cost-effectively get you right to the front of the line as a leader in your market.

All sorts of reasons to license someone else's trademark exist, including trying to benefit from the goodwill inherent in the trademark. Maybe your product would have an easier time in the market if it were under the halo of a well-known brand rather than your own unknown one. After all, which are you more likely to buy on a whim: *Joe's Guide to Beekeeping,* or *Beekeeping For Dummies*? To pursue this strategy, you may have to actively pursue the licensor and convince them that you will add to, not detract from, their brand. Trademarks are powerful things that can have a huge impact on sales. If you have a good product or service but not much market awareness, licensing a well-known trademark can pay off in spades.

Sometimes, you can co-brand your product with both your own trademark and someone else's, so that some of their goodwill rubs off on your trademark. Consider the Pink Ribbon associated with breast cancer research. This trademark has been licensed extensively by a wide range of companies that see value in being associated with this cause. Licensees pay a royalty for the right to apply the Pink Ribbon to their regular packaging because they believe they'll enjoy enhanced sales and goodwill from the positive association.

Licensing isn't an easy way to riches. It requires keen attention to detail. Work closely with your IP professional to ensure you understand the precise terms of your rights and to address potential challenges before they arise. You need to consider the following:

✔ Can you sub-license?

✔ Was the royalty a one-time payment, or must you pay ongoing royalties based on time or use?

✔ If you, the licensee, improve upon the licensor's technology so it better suits your market, who will own the IP in those improvements, and who will pay to protect them?

✔ What will happen to you if

- The licence is ever terminated?

- Ownership or control of the licensor changes?

- The licensor goes bankrupt or is sold to your competitor?

Using IP Filings as a Research Tool

If you're willing to invest some time and effort into research, you can find lots of information available in IP databases, just waiting for you to exploit it. Here's a list of some of the material you may find particularly worthwhile:

✔ Technical information to help you improve production, distribution, or sale of your product

✔ Inspiration for new initiatives or improvements on your existing devices

✔ Legitimate competitive information on your rivals

✔ Leads on potential foreign partners

In this section we suggest ways to use this information to your advantage, such as spurring on innovation in your own company, exploiting lapsed patents, or making international connections.

Technically speaking

Patent offices around the world are great sources of technical information. Fortunately, you don't have to search each of them to find useful information. Most significant innovations in the world are registered in the U.S. as well as their home country. Patent applicants disclose their invention when filing for registration with the United States Patent and Trademark Office (USPTO). Searching its Web site gives you access to virtually unlimited technical information.

 Use the information from patent disclosures to stimulate ideas with your own team — creating a new device or tweaking an existing one. However, you must be careful to avoid infringing on a patent; indeed, you may need to consider licensing. Refer to Chapters 2 and 6 for information on patent violations.

Additionally, you may find patents that are expired, either because they're more than 20 years old or because the owner has neglected to pay maintenance fees. These inventions are no longer entitled to protection, and you're free to use them.

Tracking your competitors

Using the patent office Web sites (www.cipo.ic.gc.ca and www.uspto.gov), you can track the activities of your rivals. Regularly searching the CIPO and USPTO Web sites will keep you up to date on your competitors' latest inventions. It will also alert you to potential opportunities arising from neglect. For example, are your rivals keeping their maintenance payments current, or has their registration lapsed? Perhaps they registered their invention in the U.S. but not in Canada, leaving the invention in the public domain — and free for use by all without cost in Canada.

Partnering up

If you're interested in expanding your business beyond Canadian borders, international IP databases can provide a wealth of information. Using IP office Web sites, you may find a potential distributor for your product, or perhaps discover some IP that you can license in this country.

 Many possibilities exist to expand your business. Make sure you — and your IP professional — are creative, curious, and always on the lookout for new opportunities.

Swimming with the fishes

Keeping an open and inquisitive mind will lead you to find opportunities. Consider the success of Marineland in Canada. The owners were well aware of the Marineland in Florida and California — they even hired dolphin trainers from the U.S. operation, and they copied the name for their Canadian venture. They seized the opportunity to legally establish a similar business with the same name in Canada.

Even though the Americans had advertised in Canada, their failure to register in Canada meant that the Canadians got the Canadian trademark. Although the Canadians' tactics might seem sneaky, that doesn't matter — the test is not who's a nice guy, but who uses the trademark first in Canada.

Part III
The Part of Tens

The 5th Wave   By Rich Tennant

"Well, that's all very colourful, but in order to register your mark in this country you also have to fill out these forms."

In this part . . .

This part contains some useful information in an easily accessible and digestible list. Here we dispel some common myths about IP.

Chapter 9

Ten Common IP Misconceptions

. . . .

In This Chapter
▶ Correcting frequent misunderstandings about IP
▶ Setting yourself up for success

. . . .

*1*n this chapter we cover some common misunderstandings about the nature of IP rights and how they are obtained. We also show you how to avoid pitfalls that often trip up inventors, artists, and entrepreneurs. We see too many misinformed individuals get into serious legal trouble when an ounce of knowledge and a bit of caution could have saved the day. Forewarned is forearmed.

A patent will make me rich

Not necessarily. Remember, a patent isn't a product, and having a patent doesn't guarantee sales. Although a patent makes a good product better, it doesn't sell itself; commercializing your IP takes hard work and persistence.

I must wait until my IP registration is framed on my wall before starting business

Nonsense! Don't wait for a patent before commercializing your invention. IP rights are not a licence to manufacture or sell anything; they just help you to prevent others from infringing on your turf. So go ahead — start exploiting your creation as soon as it's marketable.

I found it on the Internet, so it's free for me to use

Nope. IP laws still apply, even on the internet. Just because these rules are broken regularly doesn't mean they don't matter.

IP is only for tech companies

False. Awareness of IP assets and rights is a must for all types and sizes of business. Charities, not-for-profit organizations, service companies, and the government all use and generate IP. Even if you're not in a position to require protection, you definitely need to understand the basics of IP so you can avoid an expensive collision with someone else's rights. Something as common as employees using unlicensed software can land you in hot water, so a little knowledge will save you many headaches down the road.

I should wait to see if my product sells before filing a trademark application

Unless cash is very tight, this is false. If you expect to invest at all in marketing and branding, you should immediately file a trademark application in Canada, based on proposed use, and try to file in other countries within six months to take advantage of your priority date. In many countries, trademark rights are granted on a first-to-file basis, and delay can be fatal.

An IP right is just a ticket to expensive litigation

Owning a patent, trademark, copyright, or industrial design doesn't only give you the right to prevent others from using it. Using your IP rights to full advantage means also treating them as marketable business assets (Chapter 7).

One IP right is all I need

Although a single, well-aimed shot may get the job done, it's better to stock your arsenal with a few spare guns of different gauges. For example, to protect the core elements of its business, Coca-Cola protects the following in many different countries: the names Coke and Coca-Cola, the colours red and white, slogans including "It's the real thing," the curvy bottle shape, and, of course, the secret formula.

If I paid for it, I must own the IP

Not true. If you're not careful to spell out the ownership of IP, employees and contractors can wind up with ownership interests that make it very difficult for your business to maximize the value of your IP.

I have 12 months from disclosing my invention to file a patent

This is true only if your market is restricted to Canada and the U.S. In Canada and the U.S. you have a 12-month grace period to file, but in Europe and much of the rest of the world you lose your patent rights if you disclose the invention before filing a patent application somewhere.

Canada is an IP-savvy country

False. Canadians could do a great deal more to protect and profit from their IP. For example, consider that Swedes file 54 times as many patents per capita in Canada as Canadians file in Sweden, and in South Korea they file three times as many trademarks per capita as do Canadians.